PIONEER SETTLEMENT IN SOUTH BRAZIL:
THE CASE OF TOLEDO, PARANÁ

PUBLICATIONS OF THE RESEARCH GROUP FOR EUROPEAN MIGRATION PROBLEMS

XIX

Editor:

Dr. G. Beyer, 17 Pauwenlaan
The Hague, Netherlands

PIONEER SETTLEMENT IN SOUTH BRAZIL: THE CASE OF TOLEDO, PARANÁ

by

KEITH DERALD MULLER

ISBN-13: 978-90-247-1691-3 e-ISBN-13: 978-94-011-6796-3
DOI: 10.1007/978-94-011-6796-3

TABLE OF CONTENTS

LIST OF TABLES

LIST OF FIGURES

FOREWORD

In the period since the end of World War II numerous developing countries have employed colonization, or planned pioneer settlement, as one method of building a more reliable and balanced economy. It is felt that the traditional, single-sided systems of farm ownership and production with their latifundium and minifundium holdings will gradually and peacefully become less prominent as better settlement systems are introduced and extended. Marked increases in population pressure, large tracts of unused or underused land, and modern improvements in settlement planning are among other compelling reasons for starting colonization programs.

Of all the areas in the world, the continent of South America probably has the widest variety of planned pioneer settlements as well as the most sizeable programs. Brazil, the largest country on the continent, is actively engaged in populating the vast, empty spaces of its interior, and provides excellent opportunities for the scholarly investigation of new frontier settlement types. In addition to the academic discussion of the origin and development of these expressions of man's expansion into marginal areas, the critical examination of relatively new attempts at land settlement is a useful thing because what is to be learned from such studies may be directly applicable to other pioneer zones and, moreover, may be of vital significance to overall economic improvement on the continent.

In this monograph, my student, K. Muller, analyzes the South Brazilian frontier colony of Toledo, Paraná, founded in 1946. This he has done in accordance with the general plan and methodology of traditional settlement geography. Therefore, a primary objective of his has been the attempt to explain the interdependence between spatial organization and settlement function. Muller has, however, gone beyond theoretical organization and has effectively combined academic and applied research interests. He has been an apt and critical student in the field and has found some fundamental similarities between successful settlement phenomena in northeast Argentina where I have worked and in his area of Brazil. The extent of such similarities (or differences) can eventually be worked out only by practical field studies made by people willing to live in such settlements and partake of their daily life. In cases like this, where limited, short term statistics are available and detailed quantitative analysis is thus precluded, all the greater is the value of field analysis according to the classical principles of settlement geography. Even in the future, when more complete, long range numerical data have been recorded, it will still be necessary to employ both systems in any thorough investigation. Thus, there is no substitute for the direct observations upon which Muller has based his useful and enlightening study.

Robert C. Eidt
Professor of Geography
University of
Wisconsin-Milwaukee

PREFACE

The choice of Toledo as a study area in settlement geography was first made in a Latin America seminar offered at the University of Wisconsin-Milwaukee by Professor Robert C. Eidt in 1967. The author became especially interested in Toledo because it represented an area on the "closing frontier" of South Brazil, and thus provided a living laboratory of evolving settlement patterns within a pioneer zone. Craig Dozier's dissertation on land opening in North Paraná's coffee area, *North Paraná Brazil: Settlement and Development of a Recent Frontier Zone*, Johns Hopkins University, 1954, and Kalervo Oberg's study, *Toledo: A Municipio on the Western Frontier of the State of Paraná*, Rio de Janeiro, 1957, stimulated the decision to follow through with this topic and area for field research.

During my first stay in Brazil from May, 1968 to July, 1969, I learned Portuguese and traveled in Paraná. I was able to earn my way by part-time teaching at the Yazigi Language Institute in São Paulo. Further field work in Toledo, Rio de Janeiro, and Curitiba carried out in the summer of 1970, enabled me to complete materials for this study. Maps were prepared by Miss Marion Zirbel, University of Wisconsin-Milwaukee Cartographic Service, under the direction of Professor James J. Flannery.

I would like to express special thanks to Mario Hiraoka, University of Wisconsin-Milwaukee, who arranged my stay with his parents, Sr. and Sra. Michio Hiraoka, in São Paulo, and to personal friends in Brazil who were very helpful -- Srta. Lydia Menescal, Library Director of the Instituto Nacional Desenvolvimento de Agrário, and Sr. Nelson Pimenta of Rio de Janeiro; Dr. Luiz Fernandes Lima and Sr. Renato Mello of São Paulo; and Mr. Lloyd Strachan of Maringá, Paraná. I am also appreciative of the thoughtfulness and cooperation of Dr. Nilo Bernardes,

President, Instituto Pan Americano de Geografia e História. The many helpful officials and settlers of Toledo are too numerous to list; however those of greatest assistance were Sr. Edon Pudell, Prefeito; Dr. Wilson, Vice-Prefeito and Director of Martin Luther King Colégio; Sr. Antelmo Diel, Secretário do Prefeito; Dr. Pedrinho Furlan, Sadia; Sr. Angelo Costamilan, Maripá Land Company; and Sr. António Dewes, Escritório Técnico da Maripá.

Warm thanks is extended to Professor Robert C. Eidt, University of Wisconsin-Milwaukee, who encouraged my choice of the settlement of Toledo as a thesis topic and who patiently guided the transformation of my field notes through the writing stages. Moreover, he gave personal counsel and friendship, as well as invaluable assistance by means of his knowledge of the settlement geography of a similar, nearby area *(Pioneer Settlement in Northeast Argentina,* Madison, 1971). Acknowledgement is also made of kind help from Dr. César Caviedes, Dr. Myrvin Christopherson, and Mr. Robert Wierman.

Finally, this work is dedicated to my parents and to my younger sister.

August, 1973 Keith Derald Muller

CHAPTER I

INTRODUCTION

Until recent decades the interior of South America has remained sparsely populated. Attempts to settle remote parts of the continent have been hindered by difficult soils and climate, poor health conditions, and inaccessibility. Today, however, these obstacles to land opening are being overcome by modern medicine, improved transportation, and new agricultural and settlement techniques. Moreover, mounting population pressures and movements demand the settlement of these formerly "marginal" lands. Thus, vast expanses of South America's interior have been brought within the limits of effective settlement.

Pioneer Settlement in Brazil

Brazil, which comprises about one-half of South America's land area and population, is experiencing by far the greatest thrust of pioneer settlement on the continent. Figure 1 shows the four major pioneer zones.[1] The world's largest government settlement scheme is being attempted south of the Amazon River (Zone 1), principally in the state of Maranhão.[2] The most publicized pioneer zone lies in the Federal District of Brasília and in the surrounding states of Goiás and Minas Gerais (Zone 2). The movement of the nation's capital 700 km inland from Rio de Janeiro in 1954 symbolizes the Brazilian effort to settle and develop these parts of the interior. The two other frontier zones lie west of Londrina in northwest Paraná and southern Mato Grosso (Zone 3), and in southern Brazil in the western parts of Rio Grande do Sul and Santa Catarina, and southwest Paraná (Zone 4). Zones 3 and 4 are merging to create a "closing frontier" in West Paraná, and are joining with the pioneer regions of northeastern Argentina, eastern Paraguay, and the eastern lowlands of Bolivia to

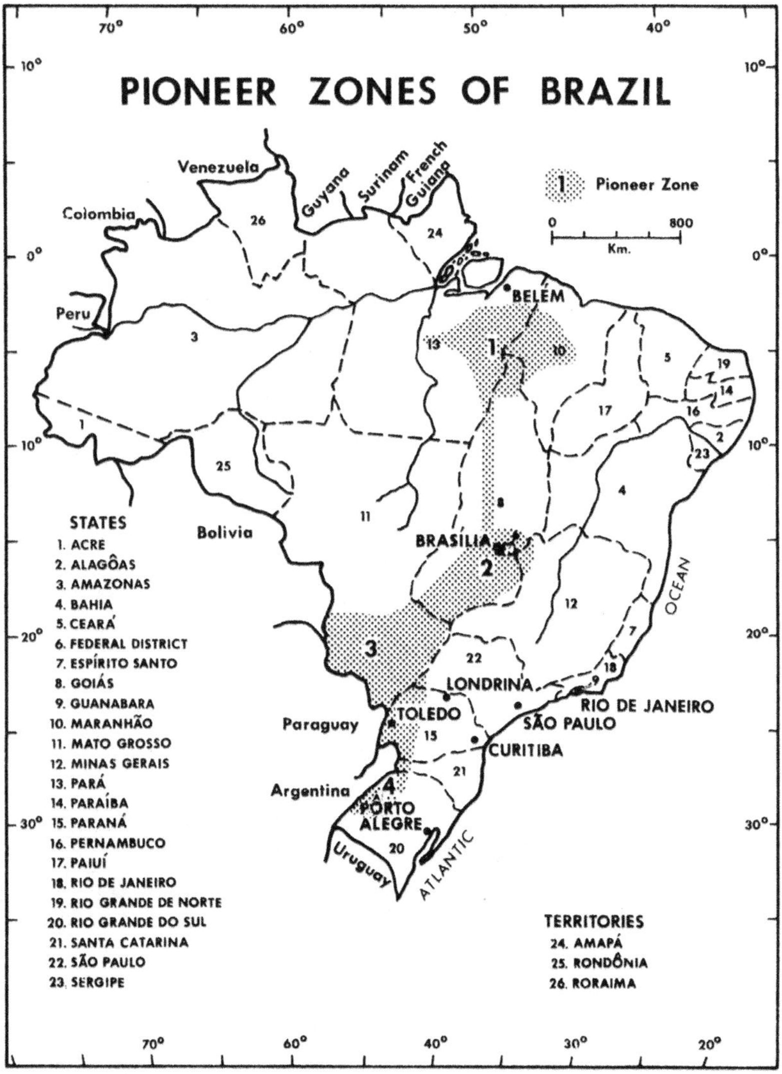
PIONEER ZONES OF BRAZIL
Pioneer Zone
0
800
Km.
Venezuela
Colombia
Guyana
Surinam
French Guiana
Peru
Bolivia
Paraguay
Argentina
Uruguay
BELÉM
BRASILIA
LONDRINA
TOLEDO
SÃO PAULO
RIO DE JANEIRO
CURITIBA
PORTO ALEGRE
ATLANTIC
OCEAN
STATES
1. ACRE
2. ALAGÔAS
3. AMAZONAS
4. BAHIA
5. CEARÁ
6. FEDERAL DISTRICT
7. ESPÍRITO SANTO
8. GOIÁS
9. GUANABARA
10. MARANHÃO
11. MATO GROSSO
12. MINAS GERAIS
13. PARÁ
14. PARAÍBA
15. PARANÁ
16. PERNAMBUCO
17. PAIUÍ
18. RIO DE JANEIRO
19. RIO GRANDE DE NORTE
20. RIO GRANDE DO SUL
21. SANTA CATARINA
22. SÃO PAULO
23. SERGIPE
TERRITORIES
24. AMAPÁ
25. RONDÔNIA
26. RORAIMA

Figure 1

form a new, larger region extending to the heart of the continent.

The Focus of the Investigation

The area investigated is the *municipio*[3] of Toledo which lies within the "closing frontier" of interior South America (Figure 1). Toledo is a large settlement area with numerous individual isolated farms and group settlements of which a total of 80 % are well-planned. The significant amount of planning in Toledo is more characteristic of the not too distant settlement around Londrina, North Paraná, which is well known for coffee production and for the numerous field investigations carried out there.[4] By contrast, maize and hogs form Toledo's economic base, and little has been written about the region, nothing by geographers.[5] Oberg,[6] an anthropologist, wrote in 1956 of Toledo's formative years and emphasized community development in the only substantial study of the project. Therefore, in 1970 the time seemed right for a new investigation, particularly since Toledo appeared to be entering a period of rapid change and may be emerging from the truly "pioneer" condition. Today various stages of development, a number of settlement types, and a growing vertical integration of the regional agricultural economy may be observed. The focus of this geographical analysis of Toledo is on settlement position, distribution, form and structure, and size, according to genesis, function, and development.

The evolution of the modern planned settlement scheme of Toledo is examined in seven chapters. The first concerns the population and settlement history and the physical setting. Chapter 2 describes the settlers and their farms. Chapters 3 to 7 analyze the roles of initial planning, settlement type, farm size, settlement function, and the salient features of modern pioneer settlement. Such an analysis of planned pioneer settlement hopefully will not only add to the incomplete knowledge of contemporary land opening in Latin America, but also will provide insights into the trends imposed by modern technology. Furthermore, this study can be compared with Oberg's earlier account and the area can be viewed at the various stages of pioneering

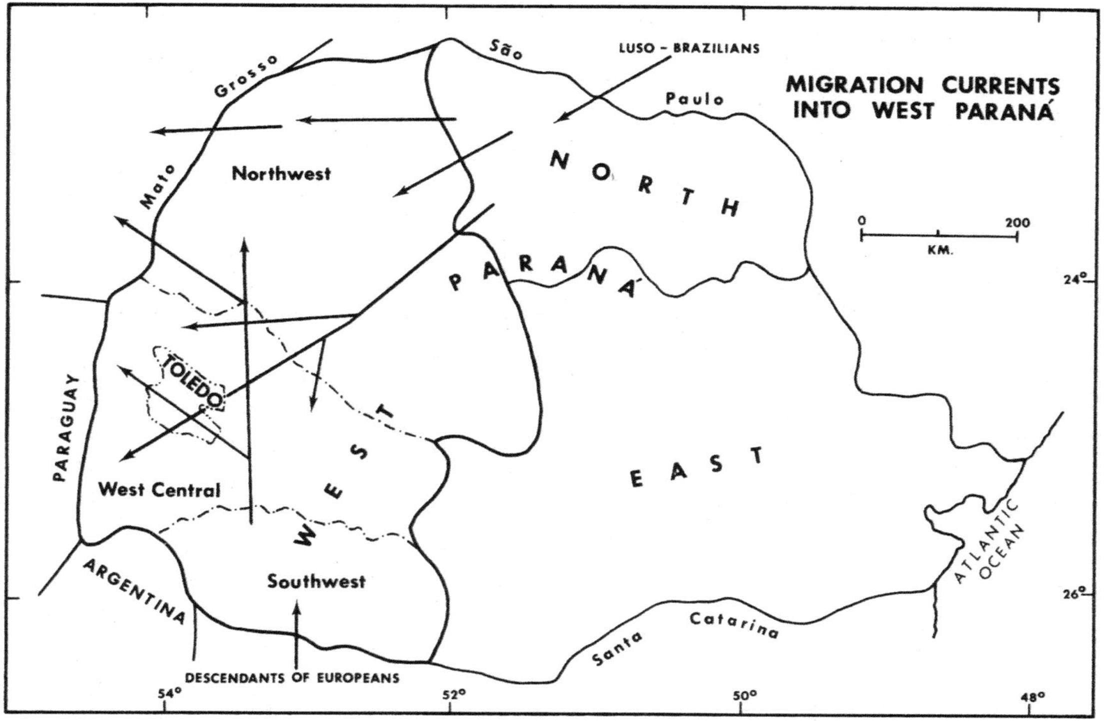
MIGRATION CURRENTS
INTO WEST PARANÁ
0
200
KM.
LUSO - BRAZILIANS
São
Paulo
Mato
Grosso
Northwest
NORTH
PARANÁ
WEST
EAST
TOLEDO
PARAGUAY
West Central
ARGENTINA
Southwest
DESCENDANTS OF EUROPEANS
Santa
Catarina
ATLANTIC
OCEAN
24°
26°
54°
52°
50°
48°

Figure 2

that have emerged during the twenty-year period of Toledo's existence. Thus, an ideal living laboratory of pioneer settlement is presented for investigation.

Population Increases in Paraná

Population growth is indicative of the importance of pioneering in the relatively unsettled state of Paraná. For example, there was an increase of 5,500,000 between 1940 and 1970, a 445 % increment (Table 1). The increases occurred mostly in the agricultural regions of North and West Paraná (Figure 2). The coffee area of the famous *Companhia de Terras Norte do Paraná* (North Paraná Land Company) was opened for planned settlement in the 1930's and its population has since grown to about 2,500,000.[7] By comparison, settlement in West Paraná has been mostly spontaneous and disorganized and has increased the population to an estimated 2,000,000 persons, most of whom have migrated into the area since 1950.[8]

TABLE 1. POPULATION -- PARANÁ

1940 --	1,236,276
1950 --	2,115,547
1960 --	4,277,763[a]
1965 --	5,844,000 (Estimate)[b]
1970 --	6,737,000 (Estimate)[c]

a - 1940 - 1960 from *Anuário Estatístico do Brasil,* Instituto Brasileiro de Geografia e Estatística, Conselho Nacional de Estatística, 1961.
b - Nicholls, *Cultural Change in Brazil,* p. 36.
c - Dickenson, J.P., "Brazil's Census Surprises", *The Geographical Magazine* , XLIV No. 1 (October, 1971), p. 60.

Migration into West Paraná

Large scale migration southward into Paraná began in the late 1930's from adjacent coffee regions in São Paulo. The Paulista plantation owners, recognizing the decline in soil fertility, began to invest in commercial and industrial enterprises, so that experienced laborers were released from the land. These people, who were Luso-Brazilians, i.e., of Portuguese descent, left for Paraná and established family-sized holdings instead of plantations, primarily in the northern part of the state. Since the 1950's an overflow of settlers from this region has migrated to southern Mato Grosso and West Paraná (Figure 2) where both family-sized farms and plantations have been established.

A southern migratory current comprised mostly of people of German and Italian descent from Santa Catarina and Rio Grande do Sul has come to West Paraná, prompted by large families and exhausted soils. Many of these pioneers settled in Southwest Paraná which has since experienced squatter problems and *minifundismo.*[9] Thus, two migratory currents of the "closing frontier" of Paraná have been converging on West Paraná.

Amidst the migration into West Paraná the colony of Toledo stands unique in that settlement patterns and economic conditions different from those in the surrounding areas are evolving. The carefully planned and executed settlement scheme in Toledo contrasts greatly with that of other parts of West Paraná where settlement has either been minimally planned or completely spontaneous. Conspicuous variations between Toledo settlement types and forms and the others are noted on the landscape. Most obvious in Toledo, as in other areas of planned land opening in modern Brazil, is the dominance of the linear settlement type and the long-lot form.

Introduction of the Long-lot

The long-lot arrangement as a major settlement form in Brazil contrasts with the *damero,*[10] or square, settlement form that dominates urban and even sume rural landscapes of Spanish Latin America.[11] The Portuguese colonial land development in Brazil resulted in less structured settlement patterns. Although land opening was often disorganized, the long-lot system was in some cases established early and thus is an old tradition in Brazil. Early settlements adopted this strip form which allowed everyone access to water, particularly along the Amazon, São Francisco, Salitre, and other rivers.[12] When European immigrants were invited officially to southern Brazil in 1824, the long-lot was introduced there by German colonists.[13] In 1875 the same system was employed in northeast Brazil along a railroad line from Belém to Bragança in the state of Pará.[14] During the 1930's the long-lot was adopted in North Paraná.[15] Subsequently, the long-lot system was accepted as the ideal settlement form for Toledo.

The Founding of Toledo

Settlement and development of Toledo was started by the *Industrial Madeireira Colonizadora Rio Paraná S.A.* (The Paraná River Colonization and Lumber Company), from Pôrto Alegre, Rio Grande do Sul. This private land development company, popularly called Maripá Land Company (MLC), was formed to obtain profits through the sale of timber and land as well as to share in the subsequent economic development of the region. A tract of 2,900 km^2, known as Fazenda Britannia (Figure 3), was purchased from a Buenos Aires based British lumber company called *Maderas del Alto Paraná.* The British company had established Pôrto Britannia to raft logs and to ship *yerba mate* by small river steamer down the Paraná River to Buenos Aires. Legislation restricting foreign ownership of land in Brazil during the early 1940's prompted the sale of Fazenda Britannia. By 1946 Pôrto Britannia was abandoned and only 200 persons remained in Pôrto Mendes to trade yerba mate between Mato Grosso and Argentina. Pôrto Mendes served as the southern terminus of a nineteen-mile railroad along the Paraná River that bypassed Sete Quedas falls and the gorge below. No roads existed on Fazenda Britannia, but there was a telegraph line trail between Cascavel and Pôrto Mendes. The first MLC truck penetrated the area along this trail in 1946. Nine days were required to travel the 40 km from Cascavel to a small stream called Arroio Toledo. Here a logging camp and sawmill were established and the present city of Toledo was founded on this site.[16] Ultimately the município of Toledo emerged around this focal point. The northern borders lie entirely within MLC land; its southern boundary extends across former state lands. Thus two pioneering agricultural zones of contrasting genesis, function, and development are involved.

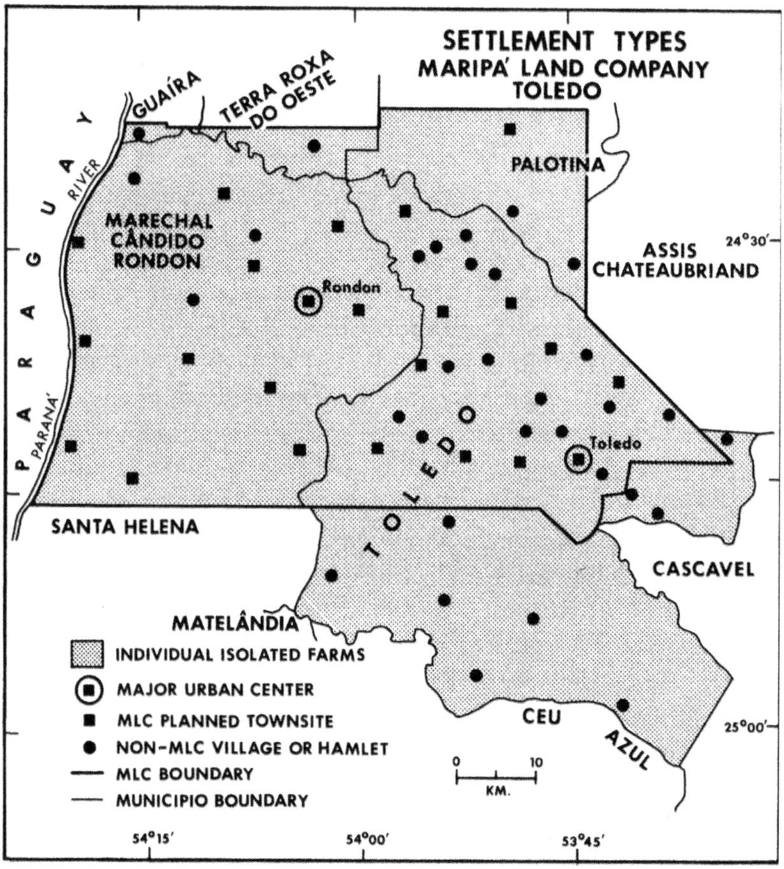
SETTLEMENT TYPES
MARIPÁ LAND COMPANY
TOLEDO
GUAÍRA
TERRA ROXA DO OESTE
PALOTINA
PARAGUAY
PARANÁ RIVER
MARECHAL CÂNDIDO RONDON
Rondon
ASSIS CHATEAUBRIAND
24°30′
TOLEDO
Toledo
SANTA HELENA
CASCAVEL
MATELÂNDIA
CEU AZUL
25°00′
INDIVIDUAL ISOLATED FARMS
MAJOR URBAN CENTER
MLC PLANNED TOWNSITE
NON-MLC VILLAGE OR HAMLET
MLC BOUNDARY
MUNICIPIO BOUNDARY
0
10
KM.
54°15′
54°00′
53°45′

Figure 3

The Position of Toledo

Toledo was established in West Paraná because of the humid subtropical climate, generally fertile soils, and accessibility by road from other successful settlements in South Brazil. Other physical advantages were the gently rolling topography, and the close, well-integrated drainage system.

The humid subtropical climate, with high average annual temperature (23°C)[17] and abundant precipitation (1600 mm),[18] is favorable for agriculture. Annual frosts prevent coffee growing and its associated large holdings,[19] thus influencing the establishment of medium- and small-sized holdings in Toledo. The climate is Cwa according to the Köppen system,[20] with precipitation significantly lower in July and August (Table 2). However, rainfall can be considered adequate throughout the year since the drier season occurs during the months of low sun when evaporation potential is lower. This relatively drier period should benefit recent attempts to expand the production of wheat which is grown as an off-season crop.[21]

TABLE 2. PRECIPITATION -- PÔRTO MENDES[a], MUNICÍPIO OF TOLEDO
(Millimeters)

Jan	145
Feb	155
Mar	160
Apr	120
May	155
Jun	110
Jul	85
Aug	65
Sep	130
Oct	150
Nov	155
Dec	155
Total	1585

a - Simões, "Notas sôbre o clima do estado do Paraná," *Revista Brasileira de Geografia,* XVI, No. 1 (Janeiro-Março, 1954), p. 129.

Data on reliability of rainfall are unavailable. However, settlers state that when "dry spells" occur in the normally more humid periods, crop yields are seriously affected. The severity of these "dry spells" would be greater still if there were not heavy subtropical dews that add an estimated 12 % to the annual precipitation.[22]

The weathered basic lava of the Paraná Plateau forms deep, porous, fertile soils called *terra roxa,* which cover about 60 % of Paraná.[23] Slight variations of this soil type occur on site in Toledo. Although the western two-thirds of the município has a terra roxa subtype known in Brazil as *Trapp,*[24] the eastern one-third is somewhat sandier.[25] Despite the relatively high fertility of terra roxa soils, once the forest is removed soil exhaustion results quickly unless careful measures of preservation are employed.

Due to uniform close drainage network and gently undulating topography, distances separating streams seldom exceed 3 km. The local relief generally is no more than sixty meters. Slopes average about 6 %, usually are not greater than 12 %,[26] and many interfluves are nearly level. The gentle slopes will allow future mechanization and have made road building an easy task. Bridge construction has also been minimal, i.e., streams are relatively narrow. Therefore, the almost ideal natural landscape makes the long-lot suitable since it provides each holding access to surface water and to a road, as well as fair distribution of soils and slope.

NOTES TO CHAPTER I

1 See Roland E. Chardon, "Changes in the Geographic Distribution of Population in Brazil, 1950-1960," *New Perspectives of Brazil*, ed. Eric N. Baklanoff (Nashville, Vanderbilt University Press, 1966), pp. 168-71. Chardon identifies three major pioneer "fringes" in Brazil. He considers Core areas 2 and 3 as one continuous "fringe".

2 *Peruvian Times*, August 13, 1971. "Brazil Unveils Ambitious New Agrarian Reform," p. 7.

3 Toledo became a município in 1951 when it separated from the município of Cascavel. A município is the smallest administrative unit in Brazil. As an urban center reaches significant size and influence it applies for município status. Consequently, in a pioneer state like Paraná many new municípios are created. For example, between 1950 and 1960 the number increased from 80 to 162. Marechal Cândido Rondon and Palotina separated from Toledo in 1960. Despite this and other similar changes, Toledo's area has remained nearly constant. In 1951 Toledo

had 2,080 km^2, 1961 2,190 km^2, and 1967 2,092 km^2. Thus, areal analysis of data is temporally comparable. Because each município center has the same name as the entire município the urban center of Toledo is referred to as the city of Toledo.

4 See G.J. Butland, "Frontiers of Settlement in Latin America," *Revista Geográfica*, No. 65 (December, 1966), pp. 98-106; P.E. Baldi, "La Colonizzazione del Brazile e l'opera della Compagnia de Terras Norte do Paraná," *Revista de Agricultura Subtropicale e Tropicale*, XLIII Nos. 2-4 (1948), pp. 109-116; S.M. Cambiaghi, "O povoamento do norte do Paraná," *Anais do Associação dos Geógrafos Brasileiros*, VI No. 1 (1951-52), pp. 81-90; Craig L.Dozier, "Northern Paraná, Brazil: An Example of Organized Regional Development, "*Geographical Review*, LXVI (1956), 318-33; Dozier, "Northern Paraná, Brazil: Settlement and Development of a Recent Frontier Zone," (Unpublished dissertation, Johns Hopkins University, Baltimore, 1964); Reinhard Maack, "A modificação da paisagen natural pela colonização e suas consequências," *Boletim Paranaense de Geociência*, Nos. 2 and 3 (junho, 1961). pp. 29-48; Pierre Monbeig, "A zona pioneira do norte do Paraná," *Boletim Geográfica* XXV (1945), pp. 11-17; William H. Nicholls, "The Agricultural Frontierin Modern Brazilian History: The State of Paraná, 1920-65," *Cultural Change in Brazil*, Papers from the Midwest Association for Latin American Studies (Muncie, Indiana: Ball State University, October 30 and 31, 1969), pp. 44-51; Nicholls and Ruy Miller Paiva, *Ninety-nine Fazendas: The Structure and Productivity of Brazilian Agriculture*, Chapter VI, "The North of Paraná: Maringá," (Nashville: Vanderbilt University, Graduate Center for Latin American Studies, September, 1969); Lloyd W. Strachan, "Changes in the Nature and Availability of Economic Opportunities in a Recently Settled Area: North Paraná, Brazil" (unpublished paper).

5 Toledo is included in a study of eight coterminous municípios: Alberto Elfes, *Estudos Agro-Econômico e Social: Guaíra, Toledo, Palotina, Nova Aurora, Santa Helena, Assis Chateaubriand, Terra Roxa do Oeste, Marechal Cândido Rondon, e Formosa do Oeste,* Ministério da Agricultura, Instituto Nacional do Desenvolvimento Agrário, Delegacia Regional do Paraná, (1970).

6 Kalervo Oberg, Toledo: *A Município on the Western Frontier of the State of Paraná* (Rio de Janeiro, 1957). Also in Portuguese, *Toledo: Um Município da Fronteira Oeste do Paraná,* (Rio de Janeiro: Serviço Social Rural), 1960.

7 Nicholls, *Cultural Change in Brazil*, p. 49.

8 *Ibid.*, p. 53

9 *Minifundismo* is the principal of uneconomically small farm holdings.

10 For a discussion of the long-lot in Brazil see Robert C. Eidt, *Pioneer Settlement in Northeast Argentina* (Madison, Wisconsin: The University of Wisconsin Press, 1971), p. 163-5.

11 In settlement geography the term long-lot settlement form refers both to the overall shape of a settlement as well as the shape of its individual holdings. The same is true of the expression damero, or quadrate settlement form. In other words, the overall arrangements of dwelling structures which emerge on the landscape, and the morphology of individual structures, may both be referred to as the settlement form. The term settlement form is thus employed at various scales for the description of both dwelling patterns and individual holdings. Only the context in which it is used will reveal exactly what is meant.

12 T. Lynn Smith, *Brazil: People and Institutions* (Baton Rouge: Louisiana State University Press, 1963), p. 259, and his "Notes on Population and Social Organization in the Central Portion of the São Grancisco Valley," *Inter-American Economic Affairs,* I (1957), p. 50.

13 See Eidt, *Pioneer Settlement in Northeast Argentina,* p. 8.

14 António Rocha Penteado, *Problemas da Colonização e de Uso da Terra no Região Bragantina do Estado Pará* (Lisboa: Junta de Investigações do Ultramar; Centro de estudos Vasco da Gama no Sociedade de Geografia de Lisboa, 1968), pp. 68-98.

15 Dozier, *Geographical Review,* p. 318-33.

16 Oberg, p. 19.

17 Elfes, p. 10.

18 Ruth Mattos Almeida Simões, "Notas sôbre o clima do estado do Paraná," *Revista Brasileira de Geografia,* XVI, No. 1 (Janeiro-Março, 1954), p. 127.

19 Oberg, p. 59.

20 Robert C. Eidt, "The Climatology of South America, "*Biogeography and Ecology in South America,* ed. et al E.J. Fittkau (The Hague, Netherlands, Dr. W. Junk N.V., Publishers, 1968), p. 71-72. Also, available in Reprint Form -- "The Climatology of South America," Latin American Center Pamphlet Series, Pamphlet No. 5 (Milwaukee: University of Wisconsin-Milwaukee, 1968), pp. 71-72.

21 Interview with Director of the *Banco do Brasil* in Toledo, Nilton A.C. Arruda, August 3, 1970. Arruda estimated that about 19,000 ha of wheat were to be planted in the 1970-71 season compared to 7,000 ha in 1969-70 in the four municípios of Toledo, Palotino, Marechal Cândido Rondon, and Assis Chateaubriand.

22 Eidt, *Pioneer Settlement in Northeast Argentina,* p. 12.

23 Charles Laurence Baker, "The Lava Field of the Paraná Basin, South America," *Journal of Geology,* XXXI (1923), pp. 66-79, esp. pp. 75-78.

24 Eidt, *Pioneer Settlement in Northeast Argentina,* p. 221.

25 From a sketch map provided by the municipal goverment of Toledo.

26 Data compiled by the author from a topographic map of Toledo prepared by the *Directoria do Servico Geografia, Ministério da Guerra, Brasil* surveyed in 1955 and edited in 1957.

CHAPTER II

SETTLERS AND THEIR FARMS

By far the most numerous settlements in Toledo are individual isolated pioneer farms. The Maripá Land Company (MLC) chose settlers primarily from Santa Catarina and Rio Grande do Sul who were second, third, and fourth generation descendants of Germans and Italians. The choice was a paramount element in this pioneer colonization. Smaller groups of Japanese and Polish descendants have also settled in Toledo. Just beyond the MLC boundary and in the surrounding municípios there are Luso-Brazilians who contrast greatly with MLC colonists. The differences and the influences of the various groups of settlers are also reflected in the settlement types. To illustrate this point several farm settlements are described, compared, and contrasted in the following pages.

Choice of Settlers

The descendants of Germans and Italians chosen by MLC to colonize Toledo had had small-sized mixed farming experience in South Brazil. MLC did not wish to have large monocultural *fazendas,* i.e., plantation operations, nor extremely small-farm subsistence, i.e., *minifundium,* peasant agriculture, both of which are traditional Brazilian agricultural systems. This group was the most logical choice for building a strong regional economy involving agricultural production, services, and industries. MLC could then expect to share in long-range profits as well as the lucrative initial land sales.

On the surface it would seem that the planners of Toledo could have sought out pioneers with medium-sized farm experience directly from Europe. European immigrants often have capital and practice modern agricultural techniques. However, the adjustment was considered too great for such immigrants, and Europeans would have been difficult to attract – both important considerations in an unfamiliar, virgin, subtropical region where rapid development was a major objective. On the other hand, descendants of Europeans from Santa Catarina and Rio Grande do Sul were tried and tested folk who could adjust more easily to conditions in Paraná and were readily attracted to Toledo. Their families had up to 145 years of experience in South Brazil; they were accustomed to the small-sized family-owned and -operated farm, and they were noted for their traditions of hard work, thrift, and farming as a way of life.[1]

Large scale advertising was not used to attract settlers, thus adventure seekers and land speculators were avoided. Rather, the Company recruited outstanding farmers as well as small businessmen who could provide a stable nucleus for the exchange and transport of goods. The leading farmers rapidly cleared land and undertook agricultural production. It was hoped that the initial settlers would encourage other desirable people to follow. The Company's plan was that good initial settlers should recruit additional ones, on the theory that quality would attract quality. Later settlers would most likely trust and respect the examples set by the pioneers. Moreover, mistakes of the earlier stages of colonization could be identified and avoided by later colonists, while the best features established by earlier settlers could be preserved. The technique of forming pioneer settlement areas with a core of efficient colonists with similar backgrounds has been highly important to the success of Toledo. Such colonists often helped each other build their first houses, and have given advice to other pioneers as well as provided examples for cooperative enterprises.

The fact that MLC limited its choice of settlers to a culturally homogeneous group is highly significant. Many problems may occur in colonization projects where little attempt is made to recruit people of similar cultural backgrounds. Although social differences may not be revealed outwardly during initial land clearing and planting, progress is much more rapid in pioneer zones where people are culturally homogeneous than in culturally mixed settlement groups. This is understandable because persons of similar backgrounds trust one another and work together more easily. Initially, informal cooperation speeds up house building, road construction, erection of schools and clinics, purchase of equipment, and sale of crops. Later these homogeneous colonies often organize thriving formal cooperatives. In Toledo, cultural similarity has added to the success of the cooperative formed by mostly descendants of Germans, as discussed in Chapter VI.

Lack of mutual trust, as is often found in a culturally mixed colony, can be detrimental to planned development. Eidt[2] suggests that thirty percent cultural mixing can be too high for efficient growth and that it would be wiser to form separate adjacent settlements with people of similar backgrounds in each. This is especially important in a heavily forested area which demands specialized solutions to its problems. Examples of culturally mixed planned settlements in Venezuela demonstrate that pioneers even resort to violence to resolve differences.[3]

Although statistics which would permit a detailed analysis of the cultural composition of Toledo as compared to other areas are not available, some general data indicate the major differences. For example, field information suggests that the ethnic composition of settlers of Toledo and three adjoining municípios is over 75 % German and Italian.[4] In Toledo alone the percentage of German and Italian descendants is higher than in the four combined municípios. Eighty-five percent of the colonists from Toledo were born in Rio Grande do Sul and Santa Catarina, as revealed in a survey taken in 1956.[5] The survey showed that 53 % of surnames of family heads were German, 20 % Italian, 19.3 % Portuguese, 5.2 % Slavic, and 2.5 % Spanish.[6]

Pioneers of more varied cultural origins are found on other municípios near Toledo (Table 3). They are mostly from the states of São Paulo, Minas Gerais, and Espírito Santo, and from semi-arid Northeast Brazil.[7] These rural workers, or former tenant farmers who had lived in the coffee areas of São Paulo and North Paraná, usually settle in isolation with little or no capital, practice near-subsistence agriculture, and are acquiring land for the first time in their lives. Consequently, in these municípios subsistence agriculture on minifundium-sized holdings prevails, minimal cooperation exists, and the standard of living is low.

Admittedly, MLC did choose settlers from two somewhat dissimilar cultural groups by selecting descendants of both Germans and Italians. But these groups had already lived for many years in separate but complementary areas in South Brazil, and they have settled MLC land in relatively segregated areas in accordance with their previous experience. Furthermore, smaller groups of Japanese (thirty-three families)[8] and Polish settlers form separate, homogeneous settlements, but always in juxtaposition with other groups. Despite the existence of several culture groups, individual units have generally remained together; therefore, the binding strength of mutual trust and security derived from a culturally coherent group is maintained.

An aspect of cultural similarity that provides mutual trust and security to the colonist is the presence of nearby relatives. In Toledo, as seen from a random sample of two MLC land subdivisions, called perimeters, almost 40 % of the owners have relatives living nearby. (Table 4)

TABLE 3. ORIGIN OF SETTLERS IN MUNICÍPIOS NEAR TOLEDO[a]

Origin	Percentage
Southern without origin stated	3.6
Paraná (other than Toledo)	6.5
Minas Gerais, São Paulo, Espírito Santo	33.0
Northeast	37.3
Japanese descent	4.2
Italian descent	9.0
German descent	6.4
	100.0

a - The municípios are Guaíra, Terra Roxa, Assis Chateaubriand, Formosa do Oeste, and Nova Aurora.

One might suspect that this high degree of relatedness among colonists is a result of subdivision of properties because of inheritance practices. However, field checks suggest strongly that subdivision of properties for inheritance is not common. For example, even in the longest settled area of Toledo, Perimeter 1, no such cases were revealed among twenty-nine of sixty-three owners who have relatives in this perimeter.[9] More common is the practice of children buying their own land, often in a different region, when they start their own families and begin farming. Therefore, the high number of related persons in Toledo is not a result of inheritance practices, but rather results from related pioneers who came from South Brazil and who wished to settle near each other.

TABLE 4. RELATEDNESS AMONG OWNERS, TOLEDO

	No. of Owners	No. and % of Related Owners	No. of Surnames	No. of Surnames Among Related Owners
Perimeter 1	63	29 (46.0 %)	31	8
Perimeter 30	35	9 (25.7 %)	28	4
Total	98	38 (38.8 %)	59	12

Despite the homogeneity among colonists in Toledo some differences are discernable. Descriptions of individual farms can give insights into the variety of settlers and settlement types. For this purpose, data on nine representative farms were obtained (Table 5). Farms No. 1 through No. 4 belong to descendants of Italians and a German from South Brazil, farms No. 5 through No. 8 are owned by descendants of Japanese, and farm No. 9, which is owned by an immigrant direct from Germany, is the largest and most progressive in Toledo.[10]

Individual Isolated Farm Type: Italian Examples

João Sandri (No. 1) came to Toledo in 1949, lived on another farm until 1954, then moved to his present property, which is located on Perimeter 1, the longest-settled area in the município. The farm with its gabled dwelling structure is located at the headwaters of a stream. The vineyard reflects Italian heritage from South Brazil. The amount of pasture and the number of cattle are both somewhat above average for Toledo. Two ha from the original lot were sold because Sandri "considered the lot to be larger than necessity" to support his family and because he needed some cash. This attitude towards the 25 ha lot is typical of many of the settlers in Toledo. However, the apparent low standard of living and the fact that small farm size limits use of modern farm techniques in Toledo would suggest that farms like Sandri's are too small rather than too large.

The agricultural production of the Sandri farm is seen on Table 5. The cattle include five oxen, eight milk cows, four calves, and eight beef cattle. Most of the milk is consumed at home although small amounts are sold in town 2 km away. About 120 chickens are sold annually and some are eaten at home. The maize and soybeans are fed to hogs, whereas the manioc is either fed to the hogs or made into flour for home consumption. The beans and rice are used only at home.

Unlike the children of many families in Toledo who value education highly, the Sandri children have completed no more than the required four years of schooling. The family has thirteen children, four boys and nine girls, ranging from three to thirty-one years of age. This is large even for Toledo, where the average family has about six to eight children.

Carlos Bassos (No. 2) came to Toledo in 1969. The family lives in a four-bedroom peaked roof wooden house located near a stream. Of the six children, two boys have gone to the pioneer zone of Mato Grosso to work as mechanics. From the 13.0 ha (which is one-half of an original MLC lot) only 0,5 ha remains in forest, the rest is in cropland and in pasture. Total farm production reflects the recent settlement -- thirty hogs, four cattle, one sack of wheat seed planted, twenty sacks of soybeans produced, maize only for the hogs, a little rice and some beans to be eaten at home, as well as some grapes and manioc.

Settlement of the Galute farm (No. 3) is unique because two brothers, Angelo and António, came to Toledo in 1967 to settle on a lot that had been purchased ten years earlier by their father. José, the elder Galute, lived in Rio Grande do Sul at the time of

TABLE 5. SAMPLE FARMS IN TOLEDO

Farm No.	1	2	3	4	5	6	7	8	9
Land-use - ha									
Total	27.5	13.0	15.0	27.0	96.0	27.5	64.0	62.5	404
Forest	7.5	.5	5.0	2.0	21.5	9.5	14.5	17.0	150
Semi-cleared	12.5	9.0	8.0	10.0	38.5	29.0	29.0	17.0	---
Mechanized	---	---	---	---	24.0	---	14.5	13.5	---
Pasture	7.5	2.5	2.0	15.0	12.0	---	---	---	---
Crops									
Area - ha (60/kg sacks)									
Maize	400	---	8.0	12.0	12.0	4.0	little	5.0	20.0
Soybeans	40	20	3.0	---	2.0	7.0	7.0	5.0	20.0
Wheat	30	---	little	5.0	17.0	---	10.0	10.0	130.0
Rice	15	---	---	---	7.0	5.0	6.0	1.0	---
Beans	100	---	little	---	---	5.0	little	1.0	---
Coffee	---	little	---	---	---	9.0	17.0	---	---
Mandioca	---	---	little	---	---	---	---	---	---
Livestock									
Hogs	100	30	44	40	220	home	home	home	500
Cattle	25	4	8	26	12	---	---	---	300
Year Arrived	1954	1969	1967	1966	1959	1960	1957	1961	1956
No. of children	13	6	2	---	4	4	13	2	2
Age	56	50	32	---	31	33	62	31	---

the purchase and since has moved to Santa Catarina, but has never been to Paraná. Although such a case is not typical, it is not uncommon for German and Italian farmers from South Brazil to buy land for their children in a different part of Brazil. Land is available and relatively inexpensive, as has been the case in Toledo until recent years.

Upon arrival in Toledo the Galute brothers subdivided the lot into two separate farms. The long-lot form was retained by subdividing the original lot lengthwise, and each farm has access to the stream. Moreover, the farmsteads are only about 50 meters apart because the long-lots form apices where they meet the streams.

In 1970 the Galutes had been settled on their lot for only three years. The recency of settlement can be discerned through visible features on the property. The house is a typical example of a pioneer's first dwelling -- a simple, wooden, two-room, structure with a peaked roof located with accessibility to water. The Galute farm has other features that suggest more advanced stages of settlement. For example, a crudely designed and constructed temporary cattle feeder built during the early months of settlement is now dilapidated. It has a wood shingle roof and is made of rough-cut boards attached to crooked posts. In contrast, a recently constructed wooden hoghouse is of complex design, has smooth lumber, at tile roof, and is painted. That the hoghouse is painted and the family's house is not emphasizes that the hog is "king" in Toledo. The fields also reveal the stage of settlement: five of the total 15.0 ha remain in forest; logs and stumps litter the incompletely cleared fields; and there are few fences. The above indicates, as is seen on a number of farms in the area which have been settled recently, that the Galute farm is in an early stage of settlement.

Individual Isolated Farm Type: A German Example

Emilio Sauner (No. 4) came to Toledo in 1951 with his father, and in 1966 moved to the present lot to start his own family. A wood frame house with a peaked roof was built near a stream. Only 2 ha of the original 27 remain in forest. Sauner has had as many as 200 hogs in one year, although in 1970 he had only 40 because of the "lowered prices". Five ha produce 600 sacks of maize. Only a little milk is produced from the twenty-six cattle and is consumed at home. Sauner has bought four urban lots for his sons in town "for the future". This illustrates that parents with specific goals for their children direct such aspirations towards nonagricultural activities and that many settlers realize that their farms are too small to provide land for their children.

Individual Isolated Farm Type: Japanese Examples

People of Japanese descent are found throughout Brazil, although they live principally in São Paulo and North Paraná. There are thirty-three Japanese families in Toledo, constituting less than 1 % of the total population. With the exception of one group of four families, each family came separately to Toledo. Four unrelated Japanese farmers were interviewed (Table 5 -- families No. 5 - No. 8). It is significant that three of them have taken steps to mechanize, since mechanization is often discussed in Toledo, but few farmers have actually begun it.

Massagi Sato (No. 5) is known as one of the most progressive farmers in the region. His holding consists of three original MLC lots totalling 96 ha. Sato's household is comprised of his wife, four children, a grandfather, and two single brothers aged twenty-two and twenty-four who work full-time on the farm and attend evening high school classes.

In an attempt to apply modern agricultural methods Sato has cleared 24 ha for mechanization and he plans to clear another 60 ha over a five-year period in order to have an entirely mechanized farm. He now has a tractor, a pickup truck, a small combine for soybeans and wheat, a double-disc plow, and a 24-disc harrow. Future plans are to purchase a larger 12-disc harrow.

During the first three years of pioneering the Satos lived in a simple wooden house with a peaked roof located in the center of his holding -- an unusual site made possible by construction of a well. The present five-bedroom house is also constructed of wood, but is much more substantial. This is in sharp contrast to the houses in the municípios near Toledo, where almost all rural dwellings are of wood; brick and stone are found only rarely.[11]

The outbuildings are also indicative of progressive agricultural practices and of relative wealth. There is a large machine shed which has two adjoining garages for the pickup truck and tractor. The hogs are kept in two separate, modern hog house-maize storage buildings. An orchard with orange and peach trees is also found on the settlement.

The Sato farm is supplied with well water. A gasoline driven pump draws the water to an elevated holding tank. This water is used by the family and given to the hogs, whereas the cattle drink directly from the stream

Since the farm does not have a generator and electrical service is not available except on a few farms located near the city of Toledo, Sato plans to produce electricity from a stream. One of the other Japanese farmers attempted to generate electrical power from a wind driven apparatus, but it proved to be inefficient and was abandoned. There are definite plans for rural electrification of about 15 % of the rural properties in the neighboring município of Marechal Cândido Rondon, but plans for rural Toledo are in the more distant future.[12]

The head of the Sumizawa family (No. 6), Chodi, is thirty-three years old, married, and has four children. His elderly parents also live on the farm as do three single brothers, aged twenty-one, twenty-four, and twenty-seven. These brothers most likely will leave the farm when they marry. Sumizawa feels that the 27.5 ha farm is too small either for subdivision among the brothers or for mechanization.

The Kinzo Ishida (No. 7) family is one of the first two Japanese families to settle in rural Toledo in 1957. The thirteen Ishida children range from ten to thirty-six years. Ishida is in the process of fully mechanizing his farm. In 1968 the initial 50 ha were increased to 64 ha to facilitate mechanization. The farm has a tractor and a jeep. The living quarters have been expanded over the years to accommodate the large family. Despite having a well today, the farmstead is located near a stream where water was drawn during early years of settlement.

The Japanese in Toledo have demonstrated the feasibility of mechanization and the significance of farm size. For various reasons, mechanization has not been considered seriously by most colonists in the area, so properties tend to be small.[13] The above examination of two out of three Japanese settlers points up the need for holdings larger than the original 25 ha MLC lot if mechanization is to be implemented. As noted above, Sumizawa (No. 6) considers mechanization out of the question because his 27.5 ha farm is too small.

Takeshi Takano (No. 8) has thought of mechanizing, and his 62.5 ha property is large enough. But he feels incompetent to undertake it. Takano's father, who died recently, made an initial purchase of two lots in order to set land aside for his sons. This illustrates an attempt to secure enough land for future use of heirs or to allow for possible future mechanization. Takano shares the farm with his twenty-five year old bachelor brother, and because of their father's foresight the property can be divided into two farms when the younger brother weds. However, admittedly each half probably would be too small for mechanization.

Sato (No. 5) and Ishida (No. 7) are in the process of mechanizing, and both have over 50 ha, Sato almost 100. Ishida admits that without land additional to his present 64.5 ha, there would not be enough to support any of his children who might marry and wish to stay on the farm.

Besides varied farm sizes, the Japanese have an assortment of house sizes and designs which are unique to Toledo. For example, the Japanese houses all have peaked roofs, but each has design variations of its own. A newer house shows an eave on eave, or *koshi-ore mune*. The older house has a broken-gable roof with an open veranda. One house shows a gable on gable, or *futamune dzukuri*; a hip on gable porch roof, or *genkan*; and a shed overlap peaked roof, or *sashikake yane*. All these forms are well-known in modern Japan. Moreover, each house has a variety of additions, some built onto the first home and others as separate structures. In the case of the Ishida (No. 7) family the older house is used as a kitchen and bedroom, whereas the newer, separate house provides living room and bedrooms.

Most of the foregoing examples of individual isolated farms are arranged along streams, or along roads if wells are available. In either case the houses are on the average only some 100 meters apart and make up the linear form which characterizes most of the município.

In a few scattered places where individual farmyards are built much closer together because of grouping around the headwaters of a stream, or where subdivision of lots has occurred, the settlement form changes and becomes a small group settlement type. However, there is no administrative function within these clustered settlements which would make them different from the individual isolated type.

In one case, a more "authentic" group settlement does occur.

Group Settlement Farm Type: A German Immigrant Example

Esenberg (No. 9), the most successful farmer in Toledo, is a German immigrant. Few immigrants from the Old World have settled in this region, and when Esenberg arrived in 1956, German-born people constituted less than 3 % of Toledo's total population and all foreign born accounted for under 4 %.[14] Moreover, many of them most likely lived in South Brazil before coming to Toledo.

Esenberg initially acquired eleven adjoining MLC lots totalling 282 ha. The holding has been expanded to 404 ha by additional purchases of adjoining land. This was possible because neighboring farmers abandoned earlier attempts to grow coffee and thus needed less land. Esenberg mechanized at the outset, eight years before any of the other settlers. His machinery includes a tractor, disc-plow, planter, and a large wheat and soybean combine imported from Czechoslovakia.

The Esenberg holding is also exceptional in that the remaining forested areas are located near streams. Esenberg has drilled a well and installed an electric pump, so a stream is not important to the location of his farmstead. Instead, the buildings are located in the center of the property to facilitate intra-farm transport and communication. The additional 112 ha purchased is separated from the initial property only by a service road. This land is in pasture or forest partly because of the distance from the farmstead and partly because of small fields that are not conducive to large scale mechanization, which Esenberg practices.

Esenberg's farm is unique in Toledo. It represents only one farm as do the other examples, but is a self-contained *group* settlement. The most conspicious features are the houses for fifteen workers' families, strung along a path located about 150 meters from the owner's house. Each family is allowed about one-half ha to raise subsistence crops and is expected to provide labor in return. In addition to the workers' homes there are machine sheds, seldom seen in Toledo, and a guest house and swimming pool, unique features in the farmsteads of the município.

Equally unusual for Toledo, Esenberg's farm is somewhat like a traditional Brazilian fazenda, i.e., the holding is large and families live and work for the proprieter. However, the farm differs from a fazenda in its diversified rather than monocultural economy. Therefore, Esenberg operates an almost European or North American style farm except that families live and work on the property. This contrasts greatly with the much smaller family-owned and -operated farms typical of Toledo.

Crop and livestock production on Esenberg's farm is also atypical. Wheat for seed is the speciality, maize is produced to feed the 400 to 500 hogs raised annually; soybeans are produced; and there are also 300 beef cattle that feed on pasture and some maize. Plans for expansion include doubling the area in crops. Most of the land for expansion will come from the 150 ha of the present property's forest land rather than through purchases of more land.

In addition to managing his farm Esenberg is extremely active in attempts to organize a cooperative. He has not become an official because he feels that the other members would rely too heavily on his leadership and that they would gain greater self-confidence and independence if he stayed in the background. Moreover, Esenberg is active in state politics and is widely traveled, going to Europe about every two years. The new cooperative has received a loan from a West German government agency mostly through his influence. Esenberg strongly supports local schools, since he considers education the key to the future development of the region. His example illustrates the benefits derived when a few colonists of great personal abilities are encouraged to join larger homogeneous groups in the formation of settlement on the frontier.

Conclusion

The preceding observations on some settlers and their farms reveal that policy on selection of settlers can effect the evolution of certain settlement types.

MLC's policy was to attract people of German and Italian descent from South Brazil. They had the reputation for hard work and perseverance and could be expected to adjust to the harsh conditions of pioneering. The selection of culturally homogeneous colonists provided an atmosphere of mutual trust and security and fostered rapid and harmonious development of Toledo. Moreover, Japanese descendants and German immigrants have also been permitted to settle in Toledo and these have exchanged agricultural technologies with others.

Single family farmsteads, each on individually owned land, are the predominant settlement type which has evolved. They are spaced at 50 to 300-meter intervals along streams or roads, the buildings thus creating a linear pattern. Over 90 % of the settlements in Toledo are of this type. Occasionally, small group settlements or hamlets of five to fifteen farmsteads also occur, dispersed throughout the colony. These hamlets are the result of longitudinal subdivision of normal 25 ha holdings by sale or from location of farmsteads close to stream headwaters so that each farmstead has water. Only one authentic group settlement type has emerged at Toledo, in which a large landowner, Esenberg, has his own farmstead along with a group settlement for workers.

Field analysis of the settlements discussed above reveal that various stages of settlement development are discernible in Toledo. During the first year of settlement, most time is spent clearing land, planting, and caring for maize and manioc, and attending a few cows and hogs and some chickens. There is a small fenced-in vegetable garden. The beginning stage is also represented by the type of dwelling: first a shack, then a crude wood-frame, vertical-board-wall, peaked roof house. This first phase of pioneering may by designated the *Initial Stage* (Zero - six months).

The *Early Stage* (Six months - three years) has in addition to the crude wooden house from the Initial Stage, temporary outbuildings such as a rough hog house, cattle feeder, and a lean-to shelter for storing maize. Rice, beans, and potatoes are planted, and grapes if the settler is Italian. About 50 % of the forest is cleared. Orange, peach, and banana plantings are started. Fences of piled logs are built.

When over 75 % of the forest is cleared the *Intermediate Stage* (two - ten years) is reached. During this stage either additions are built onto the old house or a new, separate house is built. A large, well-constructed hog house replaces the earlier temporary one. The fencing is improved, often with barbed wire. Commercial crops and livestock become increasingly important, replacing the initial quasi-subsistence agriculture.

In the *Advanced Stage* (ten - twenty years) the house and outbuildings have reached maximum growth. The forest is completely cleared except for small areas set aside for wood and fuel. Only a few rotted tree trunks remain in the fields. The Esenberg property is the only one that could be classified in this stage, and even here there is uncleared forest land. The rapid movement through all the stages has been possible because Esenberg has capital for machinery and hired workers.

When a farm does not advance through the stages in the designated time periods it can be considered in a state of *Stagnation*. Moreover, the pioneering process could be halted if a new element were added, such as soil depletion or if farms were consolidated to form large cattle operations. It is noteworthy that colonists in Toledo generally have advanced through the pioneering stages more rapidly than settlers in some nearby municípios: an indication that better than average colonists are involved. In fact, farms outside Toledo often experience *Stagnation* in the Early or Intermediate stages.

The dominant settlement types in Toledo, line settlements with individual farmsteads and small group settlements, should persist. However, changes in land use are occurring which will bring about growth of an even more mixed settlement type characteristic of more mature agricultural regions. Rising land prices will also induce the less successful settlers to sell and move to other pioneer zones. This phenomenon will result in future growth of farm size, at least in some cases. The group settlement type probably will therefore replace some of the individual isolated types because workers will live on the large landowners' farmsteads.

NOTES TO CHAPTER II

1 The basic plans of colonization ("Plano de Colonização") were written by Ondy Helio Niederauer, business manager, and approved by MLC directors Willy Barth and Egon Werner Bercht, June 1955. See also Oberg, pp. 19-30.

2 Eidt, *Pioneer Settlement in Northeast Argentina,* p. 115.

3 Mercedes Fermín Gómez, "The Orinoco Basin: A Geographic Unit" (unpublished doctoral dissertation, Boston University, 1965), pp. 265-67.

4 Elfes, p. 29.

5 Oberg, p. 36.

6 *Ibid.*

7 Elfes, pp. 13-14.

8 Interview with Massagi Sato, farmer, on August 4, 1970.

9 Sale of MLC lots began in 1948.

10 Personal interviews with colonists occurred from July 29 to August 14, 1970.

11 Elfes, p. 20.

12 Elfes, p. 19.

13 See Chapters IV and V.

14 Oberg, p. 36.

CHAPTER III

SETTLEMENT FORM AND STRUCTURE

Investigations of pioneer settlement usually require recognition of both planned and unplanned land opening as they effect settlement form and structure. In this chapter the term "pioneer settlement" will refer generically to the whole process of new land opening. Two subtypes occur in Toledo and in the surrounding area, unplanned (spontaneous), and planned (colonization). Emphasis in this chapter will be on the effects of colonization on settlement form and structure, although spontaneous settlement is also examined because it occurs in Toledo and is potentially so important in West Paraná that the morphology of land opening in this region may yet be dominated by it.

Unplanned Settlement

This is widespread in the area surrounding Toledo, in the southern part of the município, and throughout much of Latin America. One might think that spontaneous settlement has the advantages of more rapid establishment and minimal cost. However, these are offset by the serious disadvantages of land disputes, minifundium-sized holdings, and poorly managed farms.

An example of spontaneous settlement occurs in a twenty-four município area of Southwest Paraná, extending from the Santa Catarina border northward to the Iguaçu River, approximately 75 km from Toledo (Figure 2). Here numerous land disputes leading to armed conflicts prompted the Brazilian government in 1962 to create an ad hoc agency called *Grupo Executive para as Terras do Sudoeste do Paraná* (GETSOP). It was necessary for GETSOP to survey and map the area by painstakingly consulting every settler and his neighbor, and the agency has remained in the zone ever since. Thus legal and accurate land titling was finally accomplished at much greater expense than would have been necessary prior to the arrival of settlers. Moreover, surveys had to be excessively detailed to conform to the existing pattern of small holdings.

Forty-one percent of farm properties in Southwest Paraná have less than 10 ha, a high percentage of minifundium holdings that gains further significance because of the region's mostly hilly topography, which limits the amount of effectively cultivable land. A further negative consequence of unplanned settlement is poorly managed farms, prevalent in Southwest Paraná as well as other parts of Paraná and Brazil. Squatters build cheap shacks for dwellings, rarely improve them, practice poorly managed subsistence agriculture, and often aspire only to minimal living standards. As soils are depleted they move to other regions to repeat the process.

The magnitude of these problems is increased by the present population of 300,000. Had settlement occurred after at least minimal planning, many of the disputes over land, the minifundium-sized farms, and the poor management of land could have been avoided. Less obvious but equally serious difficulties arise over surveying, control of squatters, economic stagnation, and the formation of rural slums.

After land is settled, surveys conflict with the claims of the original settlers. Imposition of a government system of land division on previously occupied land can result in new survey lines dividing old properties, creation of farms without surface water, routing of roads through swamps and houses, and strife among formerly peaceful settlers.

Control of squatters may include vigilante action if government law enforcement is weak or unavailable. Unfortunately, almost any type of action against squatters is relatively ineffective in heavily forested areas because of costs and remoteness. Economic stagnation results because squatters often treat the land badly and accept no legal responsibility for ownership. Consequently, they often do not settle permanently. Obviously, instability rules; the squatter uses primitive agricultural methods, has difficulty obtaining credit, and induces bona fide settlers to leave the region because there is little hope of economic progress.

Despite government involvement in land distribution, disputes still arise. For example, land sales recognized by former governments may not be sanctioned by the current regime. This has occurred on the southern border of the municípío of Toledo, about 15 km from MLC land, in the *districto*[1] called São Pedro. Here state owned land which has not been developed is being sold by the present government as small family farms. This land had been sold previously by a former governor to a small group of individuals, but ownership is not recognized by the present government. To protect their claim the group has resorted to armed force to intimidate the small farmers.[2] Until this and similar conflicts are resolved economic progress is all but impossible.

Planned Settlement

When pioneer settlement is planned, many of the problems of spontaneous settlement can be avoided, and secure titles to land and economic progress are much more likely to be realized. Basic to planned settlement are the settlement form and structure employed. Characteristics of settlement are influenced by two common systems of land division available to planners: quadrate, or damero, and long-lot.

Readily accessible surface water is critical in areas where water pumps and windmills are impractical. In a *quadrate system* some farms may not have water, while others may have more than necessary. When water is unavailable in sufficient amounts animals cannot be raised; without animals the plow cannot be employed, nor is there milk for the settlers' children, and subsistence hack (hoe) agriculture not only is adopted but becomes persistent.

Damero systems tend to isolate settlers from one another -- a factor which can lower morale, especially in the beginning stages of pioneering. Experience indicates that settlers tend to locate randomly, depending on water, soil, slope, and other factors. Thus, even on a holding of 25 ha (500 meters x 500 meters), settlers would not normally be in close contact with each other, and are especially "far" apart in densely forested situations. The greater distances and resultant lowered communication retard development by limiting the formation and operation of cooperative programs, maintenance of roads and bridges, and combating diseases and fires. Also, in an effort to cut costs, often a complete network of roads is not constructed, so certain families may be several kilometers from a road. This means that an extremely long forest path must be maintained.

Another weakness of a damero system is the need for resurveying of roads, since they are planned along theoretically straight lines, but actual construction often is deterred because of natural barriers such as streams. This results in the need for new surveys, raises costs, and demands additional labor that is better spent in land preparation. In comparison, the *long-lot system* does not restrict road construction to rigid, straight lines since roads follow the land contours.

A main reason for a quadrate system is its relative success on level, treeless areas such as the Argentine Pampa or the Great Plains of the United States. Surveyors may well be too accustomed to square systems, and might find it much easier to continue their use than to change. Straight lines are less complicated than the variable angles and boundaries of some long-lot settlements.

Admittedly, a damero land division can be reasonably practical on level land if shallow wells are feasible. However, even on a relatively uniform plain, a square system could provide more efficient land use and services if changed into long-lots.

Barnes[3] illustrates such a case with the US Public Land Survey system by comparing two areas of sixteen sections (sixty-four farms) each. Each section has four farms of 160 acres (65 ha). The two areas differ in that one has the standard quarter mile square (0.65 km^2) properties, while the other has long-lots of one mile (1.65 km) long by a quarter mile (0.41 km) wide. The roads serving the long-lots are two sections apart instead of one as is found predominately in the quadrate system. Settlement on the long-lots tends to be in line form, whereas it is scattered in the square system. The saving in land surface releases 128 acres (52 ha) or two acres (1.2 ha) per farm for agricultural use, and costs for road construction and maintenance are lower. Additional services, for example electrification, would require twenty-three and one-half miles (39 km) of line for the square system and only eight miles (13 km) for the long-lots. The savings might reduce rates, which might in turn encourage greater use and lead to still lower rates.

Far superior to a purely square settlement form is one resulting from a system of land division which considers carefully the natural landscape of an area. The manner in which a system conforms to topography and hence to hydrology has a direct bearing on slope, availability of surface water, size and form of lots, spacing and alignment of settlement, degree of isolation of settlers, distance and time to urban services, and construction and maintenance of roads.

Long-lots that run upslope from stream to ridge in alignment with natural drainage can give each property immediate access both to road and to a permanent stream. Further, a long-lot system provides equitable distribution of varying soil types and slopes for each property. These are the principal reasons for selection of a long-lot system by MLC planners.

The long-lot system was brought to Toledo from South Brazil, to which it was carried by colonists from Germany. When German settlement planners and surveyors emigrated to South Brazil they immediately noted the similarity of the hilly, forested landscape to that of Europe and recognized the suitability of the *Waldhufen* form for this landscape.[4]

Eidt clarifies the term Waldhufendorf as follows:

> The Waldhufendorf, briefly, is a planned forest (Wald) line settlement in which colonists live on their own long, parallel strips of land (Hofstreifen), all of which extend upslope from a particular valley bottom toward the adjacent interflüve, or vice versa. A problem of interpretation arises from the fact that the settlement term Waldhufendorf implies the presence of a village because of the suffix *dorf*. Unfortunately the word Dorf may be used in German to describe agglomerated settlements (including Waldhufendörfer) whether or not central-place or internal-trade and socio-religious-service functions have ever developed. That is to say, either hamlet or village may be meant by the term, and only field work or maps will reveal what actually exists if descriptions are not detailed.[5]

Eidt adds that Waldhufendorf is employed in his book "...only for forest long-lot farm settlements in which linear village functions have developed..." in order to avoid ambiguity. The term *Waldhufenweiler* is "...used specifically for German-style forest long-lot farm settlements in which only a few lower order or no central place functions have developed."[6]

In Toledo true Waldhufendörfer have not been formed because special areas were designated for urbanization in a grid pattern. Thus, no Dorf is present in the rural scene. Waldhufenweiler settlements are found occasionally at stream heads, which is a result of surveying lots with apices to provide access to water, not because the settlers desired to congregate. Consequently, the dominant rural settlement form for Toledo is referred to simply as a Waldhufen type.

Comparison of Square and Long-lot Settlement Forms

In order to illustrate the significant differences between the two systems of land division, two kinds of square grids and a topographically oriented long-lot system have been superimposed on a randomly chosen sixteen square mile area of Toledo. The US Public Land Survey grid has one square mile (2.6 km^2) sections divided into four 160-acre (65 ha) properties. A variation of the US square grid could also employ sections of one mile square (2.6 km^2), but would have nine smaller 71-acre (29 ha) properties, almost the same size as the MLC lot. Table 6 summarizes the findings from these three systems, which reveal the degree of accessibility to water and the total road mileage.

Table 6 shows that on sixty-three and thirty-six percent of the properties in the damero systems, surface water is lacking, whereas in the long-lot system all properties have water. As has been noted for other places, properties on a damero system that do not have readily accessible surface water are either ignored completely by settlers or occupied by settlers of poor quality.[7]

Admittedly, surface water is not as important today as in the past because of the greater possibility for having wells. However, even if a well is feasible after initial settlement, the farmbuildings remain where they were. One might argue that although initial price and maintenance costs make motor driven wells too expensive for many settlers, that windmills could be used. However, winds are not sufficiently dependable at Toledo.

TABLE 6. COMPARISON OF SQUARE AND LONG-LOT SYSTEMS, RANDOM AREA OF TOLEDO

	Km^2	Mi^2	No. of Holdings	Ave Size Holdings		Holdings without water		Km of Roads	Miles Roads
				(ha)	(Acres)	(No.)	(%)		
US Public Land Survey	41	16	64	66	160	40	63	53	32
Schematic Square[a]	41	16	144	29	71	52	36	53	32
Long-lot, MLC	41	16	136	31	75	0	0	40	24

a - Sixteen holdings would be without direct access to roads (the center holdings of each nine-lot square section) which would necessitate long driveways across neighboring property(ies).

In order for each holding to have access to a service road and thus to a market, fewer roads are needed in the long-lot system than in the damero systems. For example, there are approximately twenty-four miles (40 km) of road among the long-lots of the sample area, whereas thirty-two miles (53 km) are needed in both of the square grids. Two methods are possible for situating roads that would provide access to each property. Roads total about twelve miles (20 km) when located on drainage divides. When roads are near the streams a maximum of twenty-five miles (41 km) is required. A compromise that would best serve the area could be reached by fitting the roads to the local topography and drainage, routing them nearer to the streams when streams are far apart, and along divides when streams are close together. Such a compromise would necessitate fifteen miles (25 km) to twenty miles (33 km) of road in this sixteen square mile (41 km^2) area. In addition, about ten bridges would be needed if roads were built along the straight section lines, compared to three to six bridges with long-lots.

Farmsteads in Toledo are generally from 50 to 300 meters apart. A 25 ha lot is typically 250 meters by 1000 meters. However, the dimensions vary with shape and size, especially when lots are subdivided. By contrast, the average distance between farmsteads would be about 450 meters on 25 ha farms in a damero system -- a distance too great to overcome isolation. Moreover, settlement would be more widely scattered because of the greater road mileage and because farmsteads often are not located on opposite sides of a road. When roads are built along every section line in a square system, all settlers have direct access to them. Often this is not the case, therefore some settlers are greatly isolated and long driveways are needed. Conversely, properties on long-lot systems are almost always near a road.

The Case of Toledo

The apparent success of Toledo, a youthful settlement, can be attributed in part to an excellent choice of settlement form and structure, to good mapping, and to secure titling. In the early stages of land opening MLC contracted all phases of surveying, mapping, and titling. However, this proved unsatisfactory and MLC established its own cartographic and titling facilities, with only the surveying contracted.

MLC planners, employing the planimetric survey method, used astronomically established reference points and boundaries which are far superior to indefinite markers such as stones and trees which can be altered, removed, or destroyed, or streams and water-divides as used by squatters. MLC did not go to the extreme of using a damero survey system of astronomically based east-west parallels and north-south meridians. Such a system is unnecessarily rigid in its use of uniform squares. A more satisfactory system would employ astronomically established base lines (traverses), while still allowing for adjustment of property lines to the natural landscape.

In Toledo, streams are the only natural features used directly as boundaries. Straight astronomically fixed base lines run in the general direction of water divides. This is easy in Toledo because the divides are located on fairly level land rather than along pronounced ridges. The two boundaries that extend from the divides to the streams are also straight lines. Four-sided properties result, with three sides straight and the fourth bounded by a stream. Thus, surveying for a long-lot system can be as accurate and permanent as in a square system despite the use of some natural features as reference points and boundaries.

Excellent mapping has complemented the surveying of Toledo.[8] Fortunately, frequent problems relating to delayed surveying, mapping and titling have not resulted on MLC land because systematic land opening was completed before settlement was allowed to start. MLC also provided temporary facilities for new business if buildings were not ready. All of this helped to stabilize and facilitate the early, usually difficult stages of pioneering.

Disputes over land in Toledo have been avoided for several reasons. First, the area of Fazenda Britannia was owned by a single group. Second, the region was completely unoccupied except for a few kilometers along the Paraná River, which included sparse settlement associated with yerba mate gathering and lumber extraction. When MLC constructed a trail and later a road to Toledo, measures were taken to keep squatters out.

Despite the advantages of the long-lot settlement form there is need to include special areas for townsites with space for future urban growth by employment of a different settlement morphology. If urban areas are not planned, urban settlement patterns in the form of line villages tend to develop along main roads. Extended line villages are unsatisfactory because business are often duplicated at intervals along the road. Consequently, businesses remain small and the quality of merchandise and services is limited. Later replacement of the inefficient line commercial street with a compact centralized business district is virtually impossible, because businessmen resist the necessary changes and farmers demand high prices for their land.[9]

As can be seen in Toledo, more desirable than the traditional line village is a rural line form with a central, grid village which provides a compact business district. Centralization of businesses makes for less time and energy in shopping. Moreover, stores are larger because they are not duplicated as often as in line villages, and better quality of merchandise and services can be provided at lower cost.

The two principal urban centers planned by MLC were Toledo

and Marechal Cândido Rondon. Smaller towns and villages were also established, so that with the rural settlement types, a complex regional settlement pattern is revealed. In the planned group settlements standardized blocks of 1 ha each, 100 meters by 100 meters, are divided into ten residential lots. The well-planned cities, towns, and villages have wide streets in a damero pattern and large residential lots allow for spacious yards. This contrasts with the narrow, winding streets and small-sized lots in traditional Luso-Brazilian group settlements.

One problem that the city of Toledo has is that many city blocks have only a few homes. This results because undeveloped urban lots are held as speculative investments. As a remedy to this, the municipal government plans to impose a discriminatory tax.

Another important step in urban planning by MLC was to surround each townsite with square lots of 2.5 ha each. These properties, called *chácaras*, are occupied by people in non-agricultural jobs who engage in part-time farming. Chácaras can be subdivided into urban lots as the towns expand, an important device to allow for desirable urban growth. In this manner the need to purchase high-cost, developed farmland for future expansion has been lessened.

The exteriors of urban homes generally have hipped or peaked roofs made of tile and siding of ship-lap boarding or stucco. The interiors consist of narrow pine strip flooring whereas walls and ceilings are of grooved boards. The better homes have a kitchen sink and flush toilets which drain into a septic tank. Usually a well-house covers an electric pump that forces water into a tank outside the house or in the attic. The back yard may have a wood pile, a storage shed, and occasionally a chicken coop. Many homes have flower and vegetable gardens, and a few fruit trees such as peach, plum, and papaya. Verandas are common on houses, and fenced by wire, picket, or concrete. German settlers prefer level lots, whereas Italians often locate on hillsides, perhaps because construction of smaller basements is possible. Poorer urban folk and chácara owners usually have houses of vertical wood board siding with narrow strips of wood to cover the cracks; pine shakes replace tile roofing; and water is drawn directly from uncovered wells by a windlass and bucket.[10]

Toledo is the education center of West Paraná. There are over 7,000 students of all ages in the município. Four high schools have a total of 39 teachers and 453 pupils.[11] Moreover, a state university is to be constructed in the early 1970's, which will eliminate the need to travel 600 km to the university in Curitiba.[12]

A busy bus terminal, a large number of taxis, many trucks of all sizes, and a total of 1,285 registered vehicles in 1970 are indicative of how active a pioneer community Toledo has become. Road and street construction is carried on seven days a week and often late into the night. Teenagers attend school after working a full day. The many activities formerly associated with the arrival of pioneers have been replaced by activities related to the expanding urban economy.

The smaller towns and villages function mostly as local service centers, ranging from a few dozen families to several hundred persons, but none more than 1,000. Most have become stagnant as motorized vehicles become more important and settlers can more easily travel to the cities of Toledo and Marechal Cândido Rondon.

The city of Marechal Cândido Rondon is also an active pioneer community. Its population of 10,000 is less than one-half of Toledo's. Descendants of Germans are a majority, and like Toledo, hogs and maize lead agricultural production. In fact, MLC has a new meat packing plant with fifty employees in Marechal Cândido Rondon, which in 1970 slaughtered 100 hogs per day. Plans are to expand operations to 300 hogs daily.[13] Although Toledo has had the advantage of being the center of MLC operations, Marechal Cândido Rondon competes for regional leadership of West Central Paraná and even West Paraná.

A summary of the settlement types on MLC land is seen on Table 7, and Figure 3. The mixed settlement types combined with the well-integrated road system of the area are distributed such as to give each farm access to local villages, towns, and the two large urban centers.

TABLE 7. SETTLEMENT TYPES, MARIPÁ LAND COMPANY (MLC)[a] (SCHEMATIC)[b]

Type of Settlement[c]	No. of Settlements	No. of Families	Population
Individual Isolated	18,000	18,000	110,000
Hamlets	30	300	2,000
Villages and Towns	15	900	4,500
Cities	2	6,000	33,500
Totals	18,047	25,200	150,000

a - The area of MLC includes the entire município of Marechal Cândido Rondon, about one-half of Toledo, and small parts of Terra Roxa do Oeste, and Palotino (Figure 3).

b - Estimates are based on data from Elfes, p. 16, and *Mapa do Município de Toledo, Sistema Viário, 1970.*

c - Classification according to Robert C. Eidt, "Permanent Settlements" in Harald Uhlig and Cay Lienau, eds., *Rural Settlements,* Giessen, 1972, p. 132, in which central place function, rather than size, is the main criterion. Thus, hamlets are not central places, villages and towns are.

Conclusion

Much is to be learned in Latin America by study of highly mixed regional settlement patterns. This is especially true of settlement systems implemented before the growth of modern linear-type services which tend to obscure original patterns but are strongly influenced by them. Today some settlement forms may be outdated, whereas others never were the best possible. For example, one might argue that the quadrate or grid form so common in the United States does not apply to a Latin America situation. However, some Latin American countries, Argentina for example, followed the United States system. Therefore, as developing nations are confronted with opening new lands for agricultural development, it behooves planners to consider carefully past settlement forms that may be outdated or that were in error even at the time of implementation. Such evaluations are especially critical in view of the great range of agricultural technology (hoe to computer agriculture) practiced today, even in a relatively small local area such as Toledo. Add to this the possibility of rapid modernization of agriculture, and one sees that foresight in planning and choice of settlement form is of paramount importance.

NOTES TO CHAPTER III

1 A districto is an administrative subdivision of a município which is somewhat comparable to a U.S. township.

2 Interview with José Borges dos Reis, *Sub-Perfeito* (sub-mayor), Ouro Verde, a districto of Toledo, August 8, 1970.

3 C.P. Barnes, "Economies of the Long-lot Farms," *Geographical Review*, XXV (1935), pp. 298-301.

4 Eidt, *Pioneer Settlement in Northeast Argentina*, pp. 122-25, 128.

5 *Ibid.*, pp. 99, 101.

6 *Ibid.*, p. 101.

7 *Ibid.*, p. 130.

8 Maps are available at Escritório Técnico da Maripá, Antonio Dewes, Cartographer, and former employee of MLC.

9 Eidt, *Pioneer Settlement in Northeast Argentina*, pp. 119 and 132.

10 Oberg, p. 32.

11 União Toledense dos Estudantes Secundários (UTES), "Quadro Estatístico do Município de Toledo," December, 1968.

12 Interview with Dr. Wilson, Vice-Prefeito, August 5, 1970.

13 Interview with Angelo C. Costamilan, MLC Director, August 3, 1970.

CHAPTER IV

SETTLEMENT SIZE IN TOLEDO: I

The original intent of the MLC developers was to establish land ownership by dividing the total area into lots of 25 ha. Each lot was to be owned and operated by a single family. However, as the area developed, private sales resulted in highly altered property sizes so that lots became larger or smaller than 25 ha. In fact, over the years some sixty-five percent of the holdings have decreased in size.[1] This tendency toward a minifundium system is examined in detail below.

Data Gathering

Data for analysis of property size were obtained from MLC's initial land sale records,[2] and official município records.[3] Local officials warned that near MLC land extra-legal property transactions are common and that records may be inaccurate. However, during field checks, no such cases were found on MLC land.

Although MLC and município records show no inaccuracies they reveal only initial and present ownership. Register of Deeds records were examined in an attempt to find intermediate ownership patterns. However, these records are incomplete, and officials estimate that only forty percent of property transactions pass through this office.[4] A sampling of records for sixty-seven lots from the Register of Deeds reveals that only thirty lots (forty-five percent) are registered, only five of these by the initial owners. Only portions of seven of the original MLC lots are registered. Factors that may account for the low rate of official registration are: 1) the custom of verbal transfer of properties; 2) the recent land reform which places the legal minimum farm size at 25 ha and thus tempts some persons to buy and sell land verbally in order to avoid this law; and 3) the owners may not register because of MLC's excellent property titles.

Sampling

Eight settlement subdivisions within the colony were chosen at random for investigation. The subdivisions, or perimeters, as they are called by MLC, vary from 825 ha to 4150 ha. Originally there were 756 lots formed within these perimeters. Subsequent private sales have resulted in a present total of 1099 holdings, and a decrease in average size from 25 ha to 17.2 ha.

The Classification

Although the present average lot size is 17.2 ha, in field investigation lots of this size are seldom found. Unfortunately, official statistics which would allow mapping of exact sizes are not available. However, sample studies indicate that property sizes may be arranged in a general classification as follows.

Class	*Status*	*Size* (ha)[1]
I	Original lot intact	25
II	Original lot subdivided once	12.5
III	Original lot subdivided more than once	8.3
IV	More than one original lot owned	25 times number of original lots

1 These figures may not be precise for a specific Class II or III lot.

The Class I lots constitute only about one-third of the total number and cover less than one-half of the total area. Class IV owners possess an average of 2.7 original lots and their holdings average 73.7 ha.

Trends of Ownership Patterns

Trends in property size and ownership can be discerned by comparing original and present ownership and comparing areas that have been settled for different lengths of time.

Perimeter 1 is used to compare initial and present ownership because it is the oldest settled area (1948). The classes of lots in Perimeter 1 are illustrated in Table 8, which shows a marked increase of Classes I, II, and III at the expense of Class IV. The number of properties has increased from sixteen to sixty-three, a 293.8 % increase. On the other hand, in Perimeter 30, a recently settled area (1965), Class I has remained almost the same, but Classes II and III have increased and Class IV has decreased (Table 9). Undoubtedly Class I would have shown a similar trend in both perimeters except that in Perimeter I there was a greater number of initial multiple-lot purchases which were sold quickly as single 25 ha lots. The number of properties in Perimeter 30 has only increased by seven (twenty-eight to thirty-five), a 25.0 % increase. Therefore, there appears to be a direct correlation between subdivision of lots and age of settlement in these areas.

TABLE 8. COMPARISON OF INITIAL AND PRESENT HOLDINGS, PERIMETER 1

Class	Initial No. of Holdings	(Ha) Initial Area	Present No. of Holdings	(Ha) Present Area	Abs Change in No. of Holdings	% Change in No. of Holdings
I	4	100	17	425	13	325.0
II	2	25	34	425	32	1600.0
III	-	-	11	75	11	----
IV	10	850	1	50	-9	-900.0
Total	16	975	63	975	47	293.8

In the absence of other data an intermediate ownership pattern could be arrived at by averaging Perimeters 1 and 30. Such an average, i.e., for one approximately 15 years of age, shows the number of properties has increased from forty-four to ninety-eight, an increase of fifty-four (122.7 %).

A careful examination of original holdings from Perimeter 1 reveals that Class IV properties were three times larger, on the average, than those of Class I: 75 ha and 25 ha, respectively. Today relatively smaller properties are found on these former Class

IV lots. Forty-nine properties have resulted from the original ten Class IV holdings and they average only about 15 ha. On the other hand, the original eight Class I holdings now constitute eleven properties and average about 18 ha each.

TABLE 9. COMPARISON OF INITIAL AND PRESENT HOLDINGS
PERIMETER 30

Class	Initial No. of Holdings	(Ha) Initial Area	Present No. of Holdings	(Ha) Present Area	Abs Change in No. of Holdings	% Change in No. of Holdings
I	19	475	19	475	0	----
II	4	50	8	100	4	100.0
III	-	---	4	25	4	----
IV	5	300	4	225	-1	-25.0
Total	28	825	35	825	7	25.0

The fact that most initial Class IV holdings are subdivided into smaller properties suggests that: 1) large properties are bought by wealthier investors who plan to sell the entire property in subdivided units; or 2) initial owners intended, or decided later, to farm only part of the property and sell the remainder. Either way, large properties are generally short lived; they become subdivided, and with different owners. Conversely, initial 25 ha lots tend to remain intact and ownership generally remains the same. There is no evidence thus far of the buying of land by successful farmers to form larger holdings. However, this could occur in the future as settlement in the area becomes more established.

Stages of Settlement

Since subdivision of property has taken place gradually over a twenty-year period, various stages of pioneer colonization can be examined in the Toledo area. As shown above, different stages according to degree of subdivision can be identified. Incipient subdivision indicates most recent pioneering, relatively moderate subdivision reveals intermediate stages of settlement, and when the process of subdivision levels off or declines, "climax subdi-

TABLE 10. NUMBER AND PERCENT OF HOLDINGS, BY OWNERSHIP CLASSES, TOLEDO

Perimeter No.	Original No. of MLC Lots	Present No. of Holdings	Present Ave Size Holdings	Class I No. of Holdings	Class I % of Holdings	Class II No. of Holdings	Class II % of Holdings	Class III No. of Holdings	Class III % of Holdings	Class IV No. of Holdings	Class IV % of Holdings
1	39	63	16.3	17	25.0	34	53.4	11	18.3	1	3.3
4	89	152	14.7	37	24.3	62	40.8	50	32.9	3	2.0
8	124	217	14.8	59	27.2	76	35.0	81	37.3	1	0.5
15	166	241	17.2	85	35.3	104	43.2	45	18.7	7	2.8
29	116	199	14.6	57	28.6	72	36.2	68	34.2	2	1.0
30	33	35	24.3	19	50.0	8	27.8	4	11.1	4	11.1
44	54	45	30.0	25	55.6	16	35.6	--	--	4	8.8
47	135	147	23.0	55	37.4	42	28.6	35	23.8	15	10.2
Totals	756	1099	17.2	354	32.2	414	37.7	294	26.7	37	3.4

vision" is reached with regard to the pioneering stage and changes in ownership stabilize.

Unfortunately, dates of initial purchases of property are available only for Perimeters 1 and 30. However, MLC numbered each perimeter in succession as it was opened for settlement, so relative length of settlement is shown by listing the perimeter numerically from earliest to latest (Table 10).

Two definite groups emerge from a chronological listing of the perimeters as revealed by the degree of subdivision (Table 10). The two groups are composed of Perimeters 1, 4, 8, 15, and 29, hereafter called Group A and Perimeters 30, 44, and 47, hereafter called Group B. Perimeter 1 from Group A, where initial lot purchase records are available, shows that all but two of thirty-nine lots were sold by MLC in 1948-49. Thirty-two lots were sold between 1956 and 1960 for Perimeter 30 of Group B. Table 11 shows percentage of area and holdings for Groups A and B, respectively.

TABLE 11. PERCENT OF AREA AND HOLDINGS BY OWNERSHIP CLASSES, GROUPS A AND B[a]

	% of Area		% of Holdings	
	Group A	Group B	Group A	Group B
Class I	47.9	47.2	29.1	43.0
Class II	33.6	15.2	39.8	29.8
Class III	14.1	3.5	29.3	17.1
Class IV	4.4	34.1	1.8	10.1
	100.0	100.0	100.0	100.0

a - Group A includes Perimeters 1, 4, 8, 15, and 29; Group B includes Perimeters 30,44, and 47.

A summary of ownership patterns of Groups A and B from Table follows:

1. Although Group A has 14 % fewer properties, the percentage of area in Class I is almost identical.

2. When Classes II and III are combined, Group A shows 23 % more holdings and 30 % more area.

3. Group B has about 30 % more area and almost 10 % more properties for Class IV holdings.

Therefore, through time it can be surmised that area in Class I lots changes only slightly, although its percentage of total properties decreases. Classes II and III increase both in number and percent, while Class IV properties decrease. Finally, the total number of properties, increases because of subdivision, whereas the average property size decreases.

Careful field investigation reveals that "climax subdivision" appears to have taken place in all perimeters of Group A. Whether all reached "climax subdivision" at the same time is not known, but logically the perimeters with the lower numbers should be the longest settled, since MLC consecutively numbered perimeters as they were opened for settlement. Settlement is more recent in Group B and "climax subdivision" has yet to occur, or probably the new Brazilian agrarian reform's 25 ha minimum-size limit, to be discussed in Chapter V, will halt further subdivision.

The samplings from Toledo do not reveal stages of settlement intermediate between those of Groups A and B. Such states could be determined from an average of the two groups, but examination of MLC and municipal records shows that they do not occur in Toledo. Rather, field evidence suggests that intermediate stages are present on MLC land in the neighboring município of Marechal Cândido Rondon.

Conclusion

The patterns of ownership in Toledo suggest that land opening occurred relatively rapidly, an important factor in the development of pioneer regions. When the "pioneering stages of settlement" are shortened, ultimate success is more likely because a viable commercial agricultural economy has a greater chance of developing. On the other hand, development has not been so rapid in Toledo that serious negative elements have been influential. Hurried land opening may be accompanied by insufficient or complete lack of planning, but this was not the case in Toledo.

Where there is prolonged pioneering, as mentioned in Chapter

III, the likelihood that subsistence agriculture will predominate is increased. Soon after the first several perimeters were established in Toledo they advanced rapidly beyond the "pioneer stages". Thus a sound example was established, which was followed by subsequent perimeters. The latter were able to learn from previous mistakes. Consequently the speed at which land opening has occurred in Toledo might be considered optimal, considering the relative success of this colonization project.

The processes of pioneering may be thought of as occurring in a "continuum of maturation". The degree of success of early stages affects greatly the "maximum level of economic maturity". For example, if pioneer settlement is too prolonged the maximum level of maturity may be very low. The preferable speed is that which promotes most rapidly a high maximum level of economic maturity. The case of Toledo suggests that the ideal rate of progress should maintain the initial objectives of the colonization scheme. As Eidt[5] states, "...once a land use system is established... all subsequent development is influenced along similar lines, since expansion tends to conform to the original model." When it appears that rapid growth and progress are not taking place, measures should be applied to encourage them.

NOTES TO CHAPTER IV

1 See Table 8; Classes II and III comprise 69.8 % of the holdings sampled.

2 These records were furnished by Angelo C. Costamilan, a director of MLC, August 3, 1970.

3 Property ownership records were obtained from the *Prefeitura Municipal de Toledo*, Egon Pudell, *Prefeito* (mayor).

4 Interview with Norçi dos Santos, assistant to the director Dr. Haroldo L. Hamilton, *Registro de Imóveis*, Toledo, August 5, 1970.

5 Eidt, *Pioneer Settlement in Northeast Argentina*, p. 206.

CHAPTER V

SETTLEMENT SIZE IN TOLEDO: II

Farm size, like farm morphology, is a basic ingredient of settlement analysis. Since farm sizes have begun to change markedly in Toledo, further examination of this important element is offered. Normally, farm size depends on two basic factors: the alternatives of labor, capital, and land; and the objectives of agricultural development for a given region. This chapter attempts to analyze these factors in order to suggest an optimum farm size for settlements like Toledo.

Alternatives

A general factor affecting farm size is the choice of alternatives in application of labor and capital to land. In some places farm size may be stable, so only through greater use of labor and capital can agricultural income rise. Stable farm sizes occur where there is insufficient capital and land, or when there is no opportunity or desire to sell land.

When farm size is not inflexible, as is often the case in the Americas, employment of labor and capital present different alternatives. For example, in the United States improvement in agriculture results from increased spending for mechanization and improved farming methods while the labor force diminishes. The capital is best accommodated by increase in farm size. This is possible because farmers wishing to buy more land can obtain capital and others are often willing to sell their property because other employment opportunities are available.

In Brazil alternatives in the employment of labor, capital, and land which affect farm sizes are influenced by the following factors: 1) new land is available in some places at relatively low prices; 2) the nation is having an economic boom; 3) attempts are being made to modernize agricultural practices; and 4) labor is abundant and inexpensive.

The Brazilian farmer's propensity to move to new low cost land instead of settling permanently justifies the slogan "*Marcha para o oeste*" or "March to the West". Historically, Brazil's population has been clustered within a few hundred miles of the east coast. Only in recent years has large-scale agricultural penetration of the interior been attempted. Thus, due to the availability of low cost land in interior Brazil, the Brazilian farmer seldom purchases additional land for himself or his children for future use, and settlement is semi-permanent so that holdings of less than 10 ha predominate.

Farm size is also affected by Brazil's economic boom. People are often willing to sell their holdings when non-agricultural wage-earning opportunities present alternatives to farming. Admittedly, this may not be true in the Northeast of Brazil where non-farming employment is very limited. However, in progressive places like São Paulo and North Paraná the average farm size increases as more successful farmers buy land from those leaving farming for other jobs as well as those moving to new farming areas.[1]

Favorable conditions for agricultural modernization are provided by the improved economic situation and low cost land for expansion. Agricultural modernization in Brazil is in the early stages of development, but already farm sizes are affected, as seen in São Paulo and North Paraná. The federal government promotes attempts to modernize agriculture and supports research, credit, and education. For example, the government is supporting wheat production in an attempt to make Brazil self-sufficient in this crop which easily accommodates modernization and larger farm size.[2]

Finally, the abundant, inexpensive rural labor force in Brazil is an overriding factor affecting the alternatives of labor, capital, and land. This is reflected in the 1970 Brazilian Census which shows a population of 95,000,000, and increase of 21,000,000 since 1960, or a 30 % increase in the last decade.[3] Attempts to improve the standard of rural living are made difficult because inexpensive labor is so plentiful. Efforts to improve the conditions of the rural worker are also inhibited by the low level of education, and limited employment in urban sectors.

Objectives

A variety of views exists concerning the objectives of agricultural development which directly affect farm size. The major objectives for federal and state governments are to develop a modern diversified economy and to promote a more socially mobile society. To help promote these objectives in rural areas the National Agrarian Reform Institute (IBRA) has a goal of "...the gradual extinction of munifundismo..."[4] IBRA considers as minifundium-sized holdings those below a fixed size for a designated area, or so-called *modulo*; for Toledo this is 25 ha.[5]

The municipal government of Toledo views the small farm as best for economic development of the region. A recent municipal plan proposes that a special agency be formed at the local government level to re-examine the 25 ha modulo, and place it under local jurisdiction.[6] The plan argues that a lower minimum farm size is advisable for Toledo because a high median income already exists with many farms smaller than the presently acceptable minimum. It argues further that 25 ha is excessive for farming with the hoe or ox-drawn plow; that clearing of land requires too much time and enercy on a holding of this size; that since farm sizes are smaller in neighboring municípios, why should such a large minimum be imposed on Toledo?; that farmers are anxious to sell unused portions of their properties; and that those who want to increase farm size for mechanization would be able to purchase additional land from farmers wanting smaller properties. These arguments indicate that local officials advocate small farms and high rural densities to promote immediate economic gains, in preference to waiting for government assistance programs which may or may not be implemented.[7]

The settler's preference for a particular agricultural system and farm size does not necessarily parallel the objectives of different levels of government or other interest groups. Individual farmers desire varied livestock-crop combinations according to their own experience, a factor which directly affects farm size.

Some farmers are content with practicing near-subsistence agriculture, which provides minimal living standards on the smallest of holdings. Still others want to emphasize mechanization in order to practice modern technology, and to provide a better life for their children -- both of which require relatively larger farm units. Despite the proposal by government and various interest groups of carefully considered objectives and programs, the settler often resists change, does not perceive the possibilities for improvement, or reverts naturally to his former habits. For example, even though MLC considered the 25 ha lot ideal for developing a sound regional economy, and the federal government legislated to this effect for Toledo, sizes are decreasing below the minimum and approaching those found in South Brazil, the former home of many of Toledo's settlers.

Problems Related to Small Farm Size

A serious consequence of the small property is that it inhibits the permanent success of a colony because of undesirable branch settlements which arise. As children become of age, they desire to start their own farms. This often necessitates moving away from the mother colony. Purchases of land are made at considerable distances when nearby land is not available. This is not done by preference, but because of the small holdings in the mother colony. When children have to leave home they have three choices: to farm in other planned settlements; to farm in their own new settlements; or to seek employment in a city. If they choose to make their own branch settlements, they most likely will be the same as the mother colony, and the end result may be a whole series of inefficient farm colonies. A larger initial property size would tend to avert this problem, judging from the tendency of settlers to respect what has been learned in mother colonies.

Further problems stem from prevailing official attitudes toward lot sizes. Two factors are popularly believed important: that each farm should not have more land than can be cultivated, and that there is a minimum economic farm size. Planning agencies too often restrict their thinking by only allocating enough land for a family to make a living and often little consideration is given to possible changes requiring larger acreages such as land for children and for accommodation of more advanced farming techniques. As seen in Chapter III, small properties cause inefficient land use, primitive farming methods, soil erosion, loss of soil fertility, and a generally undesirable agricultural economy and society. The fear that an initially excessive amount of land per farm is wasteful may be unfounded, particularly if settlement develops at a rapid rate during the initial stages. In fact, extra land would best meet the expanding needs of an area such as Toledo where beef and milk cattle, so badly needed but seldom seen, could contribute to a better balanced economy. Soil fertility would be better maintained, and land would be available for the farmers' children.

The 25 ha size is unrealistic. This is based on changes that are presently taking place in Toledo such as subdivision of lots into very small units and lack of attention to future needs. The conclusion is that the 25 ha farm is too small for long-term mechanization and that something closer to 50 ha would be more realistic in Toledo today, and would have been during initial MLC planning. Furthermore, experienced authorities in Argentina and Venezuela, state that small farms limit development of commercial agriculture.[8]

Problems Related to Large Farm Size

The strongest tradition making for large-sized farms in Brazil, as throughout Latin America, is the system of latifundismo, a system of tenure in which a few wealthy landowners maintain control over the rural masses. Control is exercised by keeping the rural worker landless, uneducated, and living in substandard conditions. The rural laborer takes little pride in the land and his work, both of which belong to someone else. The landowner values land for prestige and social position and regards the worker as an inexpensive source of labor. Consequently, agricultural production is inefficient and low. In Brazil, latifundismo is most prevalent in the Northeast where cattle raising, sugar plantations and widespread subsistence agriculture predominate.

A somewhat different form of latifundismo is found in central Brazil. Here, where commercial coffee farms are important, the worker is often a semi-independent wage earner, not strongly attached to one landowner as in Northeast Brazil. Because of this relative independence, some laborers have been able to save money to purchase land despite depressed economic conditions. These rural wage earners comprise the nucleus for the family-owned and -operated farms in North Paraná.

Still another form of large landholding, the family-owned and -operated farm, consolidated to raise cattle, is developing in North Paraná.[9] Cattle operations demand extensive land use, so larger sized units are needed. Consolidation occurs because farmers are willing to sell their land as soils become depleted and the wealthier landowners offer attractive prices. Some of the farmers sell out to buy land in new areas, only to continue the same cycle -- open new land, establish family-owned and -operated farms, and then as the soil wears out, sell the farms to cattlemen. Others seek employment once again as rural laborers or move to the large cities; in either case opportunities are limited and for most the standard of living does not improve. The many unemployed families wandering along the roads throughout Paraná evince the recent consolidation of farms in North Paraná.

Large farm size in Brazil, whether related to recent farm consolidation in Paraná or latifundismo in other parts of Brazil, benefits only a minority of the agrarian society. Moreover, food production is not increased and the overall economy remains stagnant. Thus, it appears that an agricultural structure based on the large-sized farm may not be appropriate for Brazil. Medium-sized farms would provide higher agricultural production and improve living standards for a greater proportion of the rural populace, and thus should be promoted.

Steps to Establish the Medium-sized Farm

If Toledo is to have medium-sized farms, special services must be provided by government, cooperatives, and private business to promote modern technology. The individual farmer does not have the resources or know-how to implement mechanization, better crop and livestock combinations, conservation practices, and the use of fertilizers, insecticides, and better seed. Special services include education, credit, and agricultural research.

Education is necessary to increase awareness, acceptance, and application of innovations. Government must play an active role in general education and rural extension programs. Education in cooperative programs is especially important because levels of technology and living can be raised substantially if the settlers are involved. Agricultural programs in which farmers are not involved often fail soon after initial support from an outside agency is withdrawn. The medium-sized farm has little hope of success without an educated population, and this cannot be created without channels for the dissemination of information.

Nor can the medium-sized farm succeed without sufficient credit for the individual farmers, even though they are somewhat educated and actively involved in improving conditions. Credit is needed to buy land and employ new methods, whether at the initial or continuing stages of development. If credit is not available at early stages, the farmer has to resort to primitive agricultural methods. Thus, it is easy to see why properties become subdivided, resulting in patterns difficult to break at a later date. In the case of Toledo, the originally planned 25 ha holding was considered large enough to stimulate modern technology. However, smaller holdings have resulted, which can at least in part be attributed to lack of credit. Thus, Toledo provides an excellent example of the diminishing effectiveness of careful original planning because further stimulation has not been supplied. In fact, Eidt's statement on Misiones now appears applicable to Toledo:

> "...speed is of the essence in the success of pioneer settlement so that appropriate methods of stimulation should always be employed once it is known that initial development momentum has begun to lag."[10]

One might add that the most direct initial form of stimulation should be ample credit, so that settlers can adjust quickly to the new region, with the medium-sized lot producing the best long-term results.

If properly stimulated, perhaps, the medium-sized farm and

modern technology could still be established in Toledo. This would require, among other things, immediate consolidation -- a difficult task. Many farmers are content with their present living conditions and consider advanced farming methods beyond their means. Others are skeptical of the cooperative steps necessary for advancing technology. Individuals who desire to expand farm size and capital investment could consolidate by obtaining land from others who find competition too difficult, or who are tempted by high offers to sell out and leave Toledo for new, less expensive land. The problem with this type of consolidation is that it takes place after soils become depleted or eroded, and large-scale cattle operations take over. If immediate forced consolidation were attempted the medium-sized farm could be established before this occurs. However, the Brazilian government has a general policy of *laissez faire* in the agricultural economy, thus making the possibility of such a change through governmental control unlikely. Immediate consolidation, which would necessitate moving some people to different areas, might be feasible if stronger governmental controls were initiated -- a reasonable action inasmuch as Brazil still has plenty of new land for colonization. Such an action certainly would be better than waiting until people are forced to move because of soil depletion and erosion. At any rate, Brazil must face the fact that new land will not always be available and that continual destruction of the soil on small properties must be stopped.

Conclusion

This chapter has shown that a *wide choice of alternatives* is available in the agricultural development of Toledo and that different interest groups and individuals have *varied objectives and preferences* – factors that affect farm size directly. The question is, what size will predominate in this young settlement in the future?

The three possibilities are minifundismo -- small-sized holdings patterned after those in South Brazil; consolidation of farms into large units as is already traditional in São Paulo and Minas Gerais and is now being established in North Paraná; or prevalance of the medium-sized farm. Present trends suggest that Toledo is following the pattern of minifundismo established in South Brazil. This is understandable because the predominance of colonists from South Brazil has resulted in agricultural methods and inheritance practices which lead to small farm units.

Although to date the trend has been toward minifundismo, there is a possibility of future consolidation into large farms because Toledo is surrounded by settlers from North Paraná, São Paulo, and Minas Gerais. They have a history of establishing small holdings and then moving to a new area as the soils are depleted and eroded. The former small properties are then consolidated into large-scale operations by wealthy land purchasers.

The present trends in farm size should be halted in Toledo, as well as in many other parts of Brazil, if economic conditions are to improve substantially. Agricultural economies based primarily on either small or large holdings often do not contribute much to Brazil's economy. Only limited numbers of people in such agricultural systems are well-off economically, and this is due frequently to exploitation of farm laborers. The industrial segment cannot develop to its full potential without a large consumer sector. If the rural component of this sector is in good economic condition, the urban sector benefits greatly and in turn more agricultural products have markets and the whole economy improves. However, with either extremely large or extremely small farms a sizeable percentage of the population is left effectively outside the economy, and economic stagnation prevails for the large majority.

NOTES TO CHAPTER V

1 Strachan, p. 4.

2 See for example Sousa, Vol I, p. 300.

3 J.P. Dickenson, "Brazil's Census Surprises," *The Geographical Magazine*, XLIV No. 1 (October, 1971), p. 60.

4 Odilon Rodrigues de Sousa, *A Legislação Rural Brasileira e o ICM*, (Rio de Janeiro: Composto e Impresso na Seção de Multigrafia do INDA, 1968), Vol II, p. 152.

5 See de Sousa, VOL II, esp. pp. 151-80, where the Modulo is discussed as found in the Brazilian federal *Decreto No. 55.891, de Março de 1965*, which is regulated by *Capitulo 1º do Título I e a Seção III do Capitulo IV do Título II da Lei No. 4.504, de 30 de novembro de 1964, Estatuto da Terra.*

6 Prefeitura Muncipal de Toledo, *Plano Integrado de Reforma e o Desenvolvimento Agro-Pecuário do Municípío de Toledo,* (1970), pp. 26-27.

7 *Ibid.*

8 Dirección de Planificación Agropecuaria, División de Política Agricola. Ministerio Agricultura y Criá, República de Venezuela. *La Colonización Agraria en Venezuela: 1830-1957.* Resumen. Caracas, 1960, pp. 34-36. Also Eidt, *Pioneer Settlement in Northeast Argentina.* p. 211-12.

9 Strachan, p. 2.

10 Eidt, p. 206.

CHAPTER VI

SETTLEMENT FUNCTION: ECONOMIC LIFE IN TOLEDO

Methods of tillage employed in Toledo range from primitive subsistence hoe farming to use of the most modern tractors, but oxen and plow predominate in this maize-oriented economy. Inasmuch as Toledo is in a climax stage of pioneering (with a large range of agricultural methods) the question must be raised as to whether the economy will become stagnant or will develop into a model of agricultural colonization complete with vertical integration. If Toledo is to achieve a high level of agricultural technology, outside help for the individual will be needed. This chapter examines present levels of agriculture and steps necessary for raising substantially the standard of living of individual colonists who have not as yet achieved operational levels beyond the pioneering stage.

Agricultural Equipment

Oxen with plow and the hoe are the basic agricultural tools of Toledo. The tractor and associated machinery have only recently been introduced. In all of West Paraná there are an estimated 200 tractors on 52,000 properties. Use of oxen and plow is restricted during early land clearing because of the great number of stumps, roots, and logs that remain in the fields. Frequently there is as much as a four-year delay between initial clearing and use of the plow. This delay, and the fact that on the average a man can work only five ha with oxen and plow, and three with a hoe, mean that some colonists prefer the hoe.[1] The plow has the further disadvantages of accelerating soil erosion and the need for pasture on already crowded holdings.

Clearing is done by the colonist himself or a hired Paraguayan. First, the undergrowth and brush are cut with a *foice*, or billhook, a question-mark-shaped steel blade fastened to a handle made from a tree branch. Trees are notched with an ax to control the direction of fall and then felled with a two-man crosscut saw. Sometimes the larger hardwood trees are spared for later use. The wood is left several months to dry and then set afire. After a commonly incomplete burn, the remaining branches are chopped off. Then the first crops are planted among the blackened logs and stumps. Colonists believe that the rotting trees enrich the soil, but cultivation of from 10 % to 15 % of a field's area may be delayed for several years until the trunks, limbs, and stumps decompose.[2]

Other farm equipment includes a hand- or ox-drawn cart for intrafarm transport. About half the colonists own small wheat and soybean threshers. Harvesting is done almost exclusively by hand; rice, wheat, alfalfa, and grasses are cut by sickles; corn is broken off the stalk by hand; and a hoe is used to dig manioc.[3] After harvesting, wheat, soybeans, and rice are put into sacks and stored either in an enclosed building or under a simple peaked or lean-to roof shelter. Better farmers have corn cribs which are a part of the hog sty or located near it. Manioc can remain in the ground indefinitely, so it is generally dug up as needed.

Agricultural Economy: Commercial Hogs

The agricultural economy of Toledo is based primarily on hog production and maize, manioc, and soybeans as feed crops. Hog raisers produce only about two-thirds the maize they require and must purchase the rest elsewhere, so maize is an important cash crop for other farmers in Toledo and neighboring municípios.[4] Over 90 % of the farmers raise hogs, but only 70 % produce them commercially.[5] At a given time, a typical commercial hog farm has about seven sows, thirty piglets, twenty-six swine, and one boar for a total of 90 to 100 hogs during a year's period. On the average, fifty-two hogs per year are marketed. The predominant type is Duroc (71 %), followed by Landrace (19 %), and mixtures (10 %).[6] Most farmers take precautions against dis- such as typhoid, pneumonia-enteriti, and hog cholera.[7] Over 50 % of commercial hog raisers feed some garbage and 70 %

buy maize to supplement what they grow on their farms.[8] The hogs reach market weight in about eleven months, when they are carried to slaughter by truck.

Maize is most often interplanted with manioc and sometimes with soybeans on hog farms. The manioc is planted at intervals of approximately one meter while maize is planted between the rows of manioc about half a meter apart.[9] On the average, a farm produces about 2,500 kg/ha of maize on 7 or 8 ha, which gives an annual yield of about 300 sacks (one sack equals 60 kg). Thirty-five to forty sacks of soybeans are normally grown on 3 ha, a yield of 720 kg/ha. An average of 150 sacks of maize is bought to add to the hog raiser's own production.[10] Supplementary feeds often come from outside the Toledo region which adds the cost of the middleman, so few settlers can afford recommended hog diets. This is an example of the need for greater vertical integration of the agricultural economy of Toledo. If the farmers grew most of the crops for hog feed and if agricultural processing industries expanded, then the colonist could buy special feed at lower cost, hog production would improve, and greater profits would be realized.

As can be seen in Table 12, family labor predominates on farms. Among the families of German and Italian descent, women and children work along with the men. Relatively higher wages for construction workers, mill workers, mechanics, and loggers limit the number of hired farm laborers, who consist mainly of migratory workers and a small number of Paraguayans.

TABLE 12[a]. SOURCES AND THE DIVISION OF TOTAL FARM LABOR FORCE

Source of Labor	%	Division of Labor	%
Farm family	90	Adult males	52
Temporary labor	5	Adult females	32
Permanent labor	5	Under 15 years old	16

a - Oberg, p. 53.

Agricultural Processing Industries

Most agricultural processing industries in Toledo serve only local needs. Many products that leave the region are unprocessed. For example, rice is processed for the immediate area but surpluses are shipped in the hull. Manioc and maize are either fed directly to hogs or milled into flour for local use. Regional soybean production is increasing annually. For example, between 1967 and 1969 the area in soybeans in a four-município area including Toledo increased about 400 %, from 6,500 ha to 35,700 ha. The practice of shipping unprocessed soybeans from Toledo and then receiving soybean products such as processed feeds for hogs from other regions, means added costs to the farmer. Moreover, about 20 % of the soybeans produced in Toledo are fed directly to hogs, an uneconomical use of the soybean. Thus a major drawback is the absence of a soybean oil processing plant. Construction of one was almost completed in the neighboring município of Marechal Cândido Rondon, but it was abandoned because of disagreement among members of the cooperative.[11]

The limited development of agricultural processing industries in Toledo results in low prices for agricultural products sent out of the area, high costs for products shipped in, and lack of non-farm employment opportunities.

Agricultural products from Toledo are often sold at lower prices than those from other parts of Paraná. Transportation costs are higher because of the greater distances of consumer and industrial markets. For example, in 1967 prices received for crops as a percentage of the average for the State of Paraná were as follows: rice 91 %, beans 89 %, maize 82 %, soybeans 97 % and wheat 92 %.[12] Conversely, prices are often higher for goods shipped into Toledo, again because of the higher transportation costs. This is especially true when agricultural products are shipped to another region only to be processed and returned to Toledo. These inequities would be reduced and in some cases eliminated if Toledo had more processing industries. Furthermore, agricultural by-products and waste materials such as from hogs, wheat, and soybeans would remain in Toledo rather than being lost to another region or returned at additional cost in the form of processed products. The lack of agricultural processing industries also results in limited opportunities for non-farm employment. This must be available or people are forced to seek jobs outside the region. Processing industries can provide the needed employment as well as stimulate a more balanced economy.

By far the most important agricultural processing industry in Toledo is a meat packing plant called *Frigorífico Pioneiro* (Pioneer Meat Packing Plant), an affiliate of Sadia, a large national corporation. Approximately 20 % of the hogs produced locally are slaughtered in this plant.[13] Its impact is shown by the steady market it provides for local hogs, the employment it gives non-agricultural workers, the skilled, educated people and innovation it brings, and the money it keeps in Toledo that otherwise would go elsewhere. The plant employs 426 people and immediate plans are to increase this number by about 20 %. In addition, truckers and buyers are contracted, thus extending the related work force far beyond the plant itself.

Before 1964 Frigorífico Pioneiro was owned and operated by a group of colonists. However, production and marketing problems were beyond the available capital and technical knowledge of the management, and the plant was sold to Sadia, which immediately invested large amounts to modernize completely and expand the operation. Consequently, since 1964 production has increased greatly (Table 13). The plant presently slaughters between 500 and 700 hogs per day and plans are to increase this to 1,000. The monthly slaughter has ranged between 9,000 and 18,000 and will increase with the proposed expansion.

TABLE 13. NUMBER OF HOGS SLAUGHTERED, SADIA — TOLEDO[a]

Year[b]	Number of Hogs
1964 (Jan-Jun)	3,921
1964 (Jul-Dec)	17,598
1965	51,730
1966	76,206
1967	114,664
1968	149,644
1969	173,401

a - Data made available from Dr. P. Furlan, Frigorífico Pioneiro, July, 1970.
b - Sadia bought Frigorífico Pioneiro on July 9, 1964.

The plant is located about 2 km outside the city of Toledo. A shuttle bus is provided for employees who live in town. The company has provided fourteen employees' houses which form a linear, single-enterprise settlement type. This hamlet, located across the road from the plant, is for workers who must be nearby in case of a breakdown of the refrigeration equipment.

The plant's major problem is that trucks are unable to travel muddy roads during periods of heavy rain. However, rain seldom occurs on more than three or four consecutive days, so the company can usually keep employees working with a backlog. The road between Cascavel and Toledo was to have been blacktopped by 1972, allowing all-weather access for the refrigerated trucks to the plant.[14] However, the problem of picking up live hogs at the farms for delivery to the plant during wet weather will continue.

Each month, Sadia loads thirty-five to forty refrigerated trucks (580 to 600 tons) and sixty to seventy non-refrigerated trucks (750 to 800 tons), the latter loaded with smoked and salted meat.

Hogs not slaughtered by Sadia are usually shipped live to major cities such as São Paulo and Rio de Janeiro, 1,300 km and 1,800 km, respectively, from Toledo. Transport of live hogs often results in injury or death as well as greater transportation costs than for refrigerated carcasses. Thus, there is a great financial loss to Toledo when its hogs are processed elsewhere.

Sadia has extended further the market potential of hogs by shipping frozen pork from Toledo to Europe and Japan.[15] This exemplifies the vast improvements in production, marketing, and transportation. Refrigeration has made the shipment of carcasses more economical than that of live hogs. Sadia has provided the capital and technical knowledge for all of the production and marketing operations. A modern asphalt road extends from Paranaguá on the Atlantic coast to Foz do Iguaçu on the Brazilian-Paraguayan border. This road is accessible to Toledo by the 40 km dirt road from Cascavel. An asphalt road continues from Curitiba (60 km east of Paranaguá) to São Paulo and Rio de Janeiro.

Field Systems: South Brazil

The land rotation system of South Brazil, some forms of which occur in Toledo, is somewhat like traditional shifting agriculture, except that it is practiced within the boundaries of privately owned properties. Rothwell[16] refers to this system as "...crop rotation within land rotation." The soils yield well during the first few years after clearing and burning the forest. However, as the soils become depleted the land is given over to pasture for a few years, after which second growth, called *capoeira,* is allowed to develop. Once soil has been depleted by cropping, another part of the holding is cleared, burned, and crops are planted there. When all forest has been cleared the process continues with clearing and burning of the capoeira, planting of crops, reversion to pasture, and the return of the land to capoeira.[17]

Among some farmers, such as the Italians of Rio Grande do Sul and Santa Catarina, the destructive process of land rotation is wisely halted by planting permanent crops such as grapes.[18] Although this is rational land use, it does little to restore fertility, and there is little demand for table grapes and wine in Brazil.

Field Systems: Toledo

At this early stage it is difficult to discern the development of a land rotation system in Toledo. About 40 % of the area is still under forest and the oldest settlement is less than twenty years.[19] Clearing has resulted only in cropland and pasture, with no capoeira as yet. Thus the full cycle of land rotation has not yet developed, soils have not yet been depleted and eroded, and changes in cropping patterns and combinations have not yet occurred. Moreover, Toledo's land use patterns are somewhat different from others found in South Brazil. The uniformity of soils and gently undulating topography allows fuller use of the total area. Modern technology, which was not available in much of South Brazil during early development, is being implemented in Toledo. The fact that MLC selected somewhat more progressive colonists from South Brazil has resulted in improved farming techniques with crop rotation and at least limited use of fertilizers. Conversely, in most of South Brazil the small holdings resulting from inheritance practices and depleted and eroded soils have caused relative stagnation of farming methods, and land rotation continues in Rio Grande do Sul and Santa Catarina.

A three-field crop rotation system is employed in Toledo with three cleared plots, two in crops and one in pasture. These are rotated periodically; for example, one may be in wheat, alfalfa and soybeans, another in maize inter-planted with manioc, and the third in pasture. The crops and pasture are usually rotated every two years. This system works well in Toledo where 37 % of the cleared land is in crops and 18 % in pasture, the rest in forest.[20] Numerous variations exist in the types and amounts of crops and pasture and the length of time between rotations. On less progressive farms the rotation periods are longer, soil depletion will result, and in all probability capoeira will take over as cropland is abandoned.

Important to change in field function is the fact that as mechanization gains a strong hold in Toledo the more successful farmers will require more land. Most likely the less progressive settlers, once they begin to ruin their land will be attracted by high prices and sell their properties to move elsewhere. This would preclude land rotation, and modern methods involving crop rotation and application of fertilizers would be implemented. Conversely, if mechanization and modernization of agriculture fail, land rotation and its related problems may eventually dominate the scene. Present trends suggest that cooperative efforts by a nucleus of progressive colonists can succeed in establishing modern agricultural technology, and Toledo may well be saved from the undesirable land use patterns that predominate elsewhere in South Brazil.

Agricultural Assistance

The family-sized farm is generally accepted as ideal for agricultural colonization projects. However, agencies for organizing large scale assistance to family farmers are needed especially at the beginning. This would include mechanization, research, technical assistance, crop processing, marketing, credit, and purchase of supplies. Lack of such aid can lead to the downfall of colonization.

In Toledo these services are available to a certain degree. During the earliest stages of settlement MLC gave much assistance and leadership to the pioneers. Private firms subsequently took over most of the early functions of MLC. For example, some MLC officials and a number of settlers formed a separate company, called *Empório Toledo Ltda*, to operate a department store in Toledo and branch stores in outlying villages as well as to establish small industries and other commercial enterprices.[21] More recently, the municipal government has taken an active role in former functions of MLC. The state and federal governments have also become active in research, technical assistance, and credit in Toledo, as in much of the rest of Brazil.

The fact that settlers brought their own working capital to Toledo is highly significant. It is often beyond the capability of a colonization agency, whether private or governmental, to provide all the capital needed. Fixed capital must be furnished by the agency for main roads, tools, and livestock, but additional capital for housing, clearing of land, schools, hospitals, and side roads is often lacking. Therefore, individual settlers must provide all or part of the working capital for these kinds of needs from the outset, and colonists with their own capital can greatly reduce the time spent in early stages of pioneering. Settlement agencies cannot allow themselves to believe that success will follow automatically where they provide fixed capital. They must provide at least part of the working capital as well, or choose settlers who have it or can acquire loans, as some of the Toledo colonists were able to do.

Cooperatives

Recent attempts to modernize Toledo's agriculture have required still greater amounts of capital. Government assistance is usually inadequate, so the settlers have formed cooperatives. In 1970 colonists from the municípios of Toledo, Marechal Cândido Rondon, and Palotina formed a large cooperative.[22] However, at the time of this study the membership appeared to be in favor of dividing the group into three separate cooperatives to allow more local autonomy, although those favoring one large body feel that size is an important element for greater power and influence. There were 260 members in 1970 and hopes were to raise membership to 500. Fees include a minimum of New Cruzeiros $200 (about US $40) per year and an additional New Cruzeiros $20 per hectare when a farmer has more than 10 ha of cultivated land.

The cooperative's major goals are to provide for some farm education, a radio equipped mechanical repair patrol, crop storage facilities, credit, sale of crops, and purchase of farm supplies such as fertilizers, seeds, and insecticides. A training center for meetings, classes, movies, and exhibitions will be constructed. A model garage and a model milking shed for demonstrating are in the planning stages. A warehouse for wheat has already been built and there are plans for a wheat mill. Financial support for the cooperative has come so far from membership fees and a loan from a West German government agency, with none from state or federal governments, although they encourage the venture.

The National Institute of Agrarian Development (INDA) has made the formation of rural cooperatives in Brazil a major objective.[23] The significance of this cooperative in its example to other settlers who will see the possibilities of improved agricultural methods through cooperative effort.

Conclusion

In this chapter it has been pointed out that agricultural development in Toledo has increased steadily, incipient vertical integration is taking place with the help of agricultural processing industries, and modern techniques of farming are being introduced. Moreover, government has provided the structure for supporting services such as credit, education, technical assistance, transportation, and agricultural research. However, there appears to be evidence that the economic development will lead to a widening of the gap between those colonists developing modern farming techniques and those who continue to use traditional methods. The question is whether the average colonist will receive sufficient assistance to change his methods. This depends on the formation of cooperatives by the farmers themselves and on whether steps can be taken to reverse the tendency of farm subdivision which works against the introduction of modern agricultural technology.

NOTES TO CHAPTER VI

1 Elfes, p. 26 and 28.

2 See Oberg, pp. 51-52.

3 Elfes, p. 29.

4 Frigorífico Pioneiro S.A., *Levantamento Estatístico da Produção Agro-pecuaria -- Parte do Oeste Paranaense: Toledo* (1969?), p. 67.

5 *Ibid.*, p, 71.

6 *Ibid.*, p. 65.

7 Oberg, pp. 60-61.

8 Frigorífico Pioneiro S.A., p. 65.

9 ACARPA, p. 16.

10 Frigorífico Pioneiro, p. 67.

11 Elfes, Anexo 7 and p. 21.

12 *Ibid.*, p. 22.

13 Interview with Dr. Pedrinho Furlan, director, Frigorífico Pioneiro -- Sadia, Toledo, July 31, 1970.

14 *Ibid.*

15 *Ibid.*

16 Stuart Clark Rothwell, *The Old Italian Colonial Zone of Rio Grande do Sul, Brazil* (Porte Alegre, 1959), p. 50.

17 Jean Roche, *A Colonização Alema e O Rio Grande do Sul,* trans. Emery Ruas (Pôrto Alegre, Brasil: Editôra Globo, 1969), I, pp. 286-96.

18 Rothwell, p. 49.

19 Interview with Dr. Furlan, July 31, 1970.

20 ACARPA, p. 6.

21 According to Oberg, p. 26, MLC helped establish the following independent companies; Auto-Mecânica Toledo Ltda, Beneficiadoras de Madeiras Ltda; Agro-Industrial do Prata Ltda and Industrial de Máquinas Toledo Ltda.

22 Interview with Fredrich Paul Heinrich Esenberg, farmer, August 1, 1970.

23 de Sousa, Vol II, pp. 3-78.

CHAPTER VII

CONCLUSIONS

This geographical analysis of pioneer settlement in Toledo represents an attempt to portray the significant elements of modern agricultural settlement in Latin America. The identification of these elements is meant to bring insight to the modern colonization process. Successful modern colonization depends primarily on two factors, the rapid adaption of settlers to the new areas, and the speed with which commercial agriculture is developed. These depend on the position of the colonization project, selection of settlers, method of land titling, settlement morphology, settlement size, and the role of settlement function in vertical integration and regional settlement development.

Position of the Colonization Project

The principal hindrance to initial settlement in Toledo was inaccessibility rather than an unfavorable physical environment, and once a road was cleared this problem was removed. The fertile *terra roxa* soils, the subtropical climate, the gently undulating topography, and the close network of streams made an almost ideal setting for agricultural colonization. The question, therefore, was not whether this location was suitable for colonization, but what could be done with it given accessibility and the right kind of pioneer.

Selection of Settlers

Many colonization projects, particularily governmental, do not always limit selection of colonists to a culturally homogeneous group. However, Toledo had the advantage of being developed by a private land company which hand picked its settlers. These were descendants of Germans and Italians from South Brazil, with much smaller groups of Japanese and Polish descent as well as a few European immigrants. The cultural homogeneity of these groups has been maintained and has been a key element in the success of Toledo. Much is to be learned from this juxtaposition of solid cores of settlers who have the same language, social customs, home towns and who possess highly developed organizational backgrounds and cooperative experience. Settlers without such qualifications were not recruited or were not attracted to the project because of the cost of land or because there was no advertising of land sales. Consequently, the groups of colonists from South Brazil have brought to Toledo special culture traits which facilitate land opening.

Land Titling

Disputes over land, insecure ownership, speculation, fraudulent claims, and squatters are all too familiar in pioneer zones throughout Latin America. MLC has avoided these negative elements by acquiring undisputed ownership to a large tract of land that was almost completely unoccupied and by subdividing the tract into individual lots that were accurately surveyed, mapped, and described in detail on land titles. Only after these tasks were performed were the first settlers allowed to take possession of their new properties. As a result, there has yet to be a dispute over MLC land. In contrast, colonists in areas bordering MLC land tell of numerous disputes, haphazard settlement patterns, and insecure land ownership. Only with a sound land titling system that results from accurate surveying and detailed mapping are settlers assured the sense of permanence necessary to contribute to progress.

Settlement Morphology

The long-lot field form, so common throughout South Brazil, was adopted by MLC for Toledo. It conforms ideally to the undulating topography and close stream network and allows a uniform distribution of slope and soils, an efficient road network, and good communications. The result was a linear settlement form with farmsteads located along roads which are generally near streams, or less often, on divides. Occasional hamlets have appeared because of sub-longitudinal division of land and at stream headwaters. Central areas for villages and towns were set aside, in which a grid settlement form was established. Towns were surrounded by small square holdings of 2.5 ha called chácaras which can in the future be subdivided easily into urban lots. Subdivision of chácaras for urban expansion eliminates the need of breaking up the regular farms. Thus, the long-lot farm settlement form combined with the urban grid type affords a well-integrated network of transportation and other facilities which are now available to each of Toledo's 12,500 family-sized rural properties.

Settlement Size

Throughout Brazil and the rest of Latin America the evils of latifundia and minifundia are apparent. In Toledo, first by MLC planners, and more recently by the Brazilian Institute of Agrarian Reform, attempts have been made to establish medium-sized farms of 25 ha, in an effort to help the rural populace contribute to a viable national economy. However, the need to increase farm size beyond 25 ha has become obvious as modern farming techniques are implemented in Toledo. Therefore, unless official measures are exerted to limit subdivision of existing properties, or the consolidation of properties into super-holdings by a few wealthy landowners, there is little hope of absorbing a large segment of this agrarian society into the effective national economy. The greatest opportunity to adopt a policy favoring the medium-sized farm is afforded during the early years of development in pioneer zones like Toledo.

Settlement Function: Vertical Integration and Regional Settlement Development

Another aspect involving form and size of settlements is the overall development of a mixed settlement pattern in Toledo. The area of MLC has 2,900 km^2 occupied by approximately 18,000 farms that are integrated in an overall settlement pattern served by about 30 hamlets (small group settlements), 15 villages and towns, and two urban centers. This highly mixed settlement pattern is an indication of economic strength and growth and has been an essential element in the apparent success of Toledo.

Agricultural production also indicates rapid growth. Tabulated data have shown the significance of maize, manioc, and hog production and the somewhat lesser importance of rice, soybeans, and wheat. From 1960 to 1967 the total area of Toledo in cultivated crops increased about five-fold, from 16,177 ha to 76,900 ha. During the same period hog production rose over 330 %, from 122,000 to 526,000. Data from 1965 to 1969 show that in four municípios including Toledo the area devoted to maize increased 270 %, 27,660 ha to 103,000 ha.

Agricultural processing industries, especially those associated with hogs, are also increasing production and have potential for further expansion. For example, the decision of a major national corporation (Sadia) to establish in Toledo one of the largest and most modern meat packing plants in Latin America demonstrates great confidence in the region. A subsidiary of MLC has established another meat packing plant in the município of Marechal Cândido Rondon, indicating the influence of Toledo's success on neighboring areas.

Despite the apparent success of the maize-hog economy, the individual colonist has a generally low standard of living and limited opportunity for improvement. Government programs and credit do not benefit the average colonist. Prices for agricultural products are subject to fluctuating markets, and the middleman often cuts into profits. Agricultural cooperatives appear to be the only solution to these problems. Cooperative buying of agricultural supplies should lower costs and with storage facilities and marketing cooperatives the farmer should receive a greater share of profits. Furthermore, the individual colonist could then contribute more to the regional and national economies.

In summary, this writer feels that Toledo's future requires much more emphasis on vertical integration and an increase in farm size. A certain percentage of the farm population, perhaps

20 % to 25 %, will remain at the initial stage of pioneering because of lack of cash for improvements. However, as more progressive colonists adopt modern technology, the standard of living will rise substantially, and in contrast to many surrounding areas of West Paraná, a well-integrated economy will result. If judged as a success or failure within the context of Brazilian national output, the colony of Toledo is certainly emerging on the "plus side".

GPSR Compliance

The European Union's (EU) General Product Safety Regulation (GPSR) is a set of rules that requires consumer products to be safe and our obligations to ensure this.

If you have any concerns about our products, you can contact us on ProductSafety@springernature.com

In case Publisher is established outside the EU, the EU authorized representative is:

Springer Nature Customer Service Center GmbH
Europaplatz 3
69115 Heidelberg, Germany

Batch number: 10830943

Printed by Printforce, the Netherlands